Oregon Legal Research

Carolina Academic Press
Legal Research Series

Tenielle Fordyce-Ruff, Series Editor
Suzanne E. Rowe, Series Editor Emerita

Arizona, Fourth Edition — Tamara S. Herrera
Arkansas, Second Edition — Coleen M. Barger, Cheryl L. Reinhart & Cathy L. Underwood
California, Fourth Edition — Aimee Dudovitz, Sarah Laubach & Suzanne E. Rowe
Colorado, Second Edition — Robert Michael Linz
Connecticut, Second Edition — Anne Rajotte & Jessica Rubin
Federal, Second Edition — Mary Garvey Algero, Spencer L. Simons, Suzanne E. Rowe, Scott Childs & Sarah E. Ricks
Florida, Fifth Edition — Barbara J. Busharis, Anne E. Mullins & Suzanne E. Rowe
Georgia, Second Edition — Margaret Butler & Thomas Striepe
Hawai'i — Victoria Szymczak, Cory Lenz & Roberta Woods
Idaho, Fourth Edition — Tenielle Fordyce-Ruff
Illinois, Second Edition — Mark E. Wojcik
Indiana — Ashley Ames Ahlbrand & Michelle Trumbo
Iowa, Third Edition — John D. Edwards, Karen L. Wallace & Melissa H. Weresh
Kansas — Joseph A. Custer & Christopher L. Steadham
Kentucky, Second Edition — William A. Hilyerd, Kurt X. Metzmeier & David J. Ensign
Louisiana, Fourth Edition — Mary Garvey Algero
Massachusetts, Second Edition — E. Joan Blum & Shaun B. Spencer
Michigan, Fourth Edition — Cristina D. Lockwood
Minnesota — Suzanne Thorpe
Mississippi — Kristy L. Gilliland
Missouri, Fourth Edition — Wanda M. Temm & Julie M. Cheslik
New York, Fourth Edition — Elizabeth G. Adelman, Courtney L. Selby, Brian Detweiler & Kathleen Darvil
North Carolina, Third Edition — Brenda D. Gibson, Julie L. Kimbrough, Laura P. Graham & Nichelle J. Perry
North Dakota — Anne E. Mullins & Tammy Pettinato Oltz
Ohio, Third Edition — Sara Sampson, Katherine L. Hall & Carolyn Broering-Jacobs
Oklahoma — Darin K. Fox, Darla W. Jackson & Courtney L. Selby
Oregon, Sixth Edition — Megan Austin & Kelly Reynolds
Pennsylvania, Second Edition — Barbara J. Busharis, Catherine M. Dunn, Bonny L. Tavares & Carla P. Wale
Tennessee, Third Edition — Scott Childs & Sibyl Marshall
Texas, Second Edition — Spencer L. Simons
Washington, Second Edition — Julie A. Heintz-Cho, Tom Cobb & Mary A. Hotchkiss
West Virginia, Second Edition — Hollee Schwartz Temple
Wisconsin — Patricia Cervenka & Leslie Behroozi
Wyoming, Third Edition — Debora A. Person & Tawnya K. Plumb

Oregon Legal Research

Sixth Edition

Megan Austin
Kelly Reynolds

Tenielle Fordyce-Ruff, Series Editor
Suzanne E. Rowe, Series Editor Emerita

CAROLINA ACADEMIC PRESS
Durham, North Carolina

Library of Congress Cataloging-in-Publication Data

Names: Austin, Megan, 1966- author. | Reynolds, Kelly (Co-author of Oregon legal research), author.
Title: Oregon legal research / Megan Austin, Kelly Reynolds.
Description: Sixth edition. | Durham, North Carolina : Carolina Academic Press, 2025. | Series: Legal research series | Includes bibliographical references and index.
Identifiers: LCCN 2025020325 | ISBN 9781531029630 (paperback) | ISBN 9781531029647 (ebook)
Subjects: LCSH: Legal research—Oregon.
Classification: LCC KFO2475 .R69 2025 | DDC 340.072/0795—dc23/eng/20250428
LC record available at https://lccn.loc.gov/2025020325

Carolina Academic Press
700 Kent Street
Durham, North Carolina 27701
(919) 489-7486
www.cap-press.com

Printed in the United States of America.

Summary of Contents

Contents

List of Tables and Figures

Preface and Acknowledgments

This sixth edition of *Oregon Legal Research* teaches law students, paralegals, and other newcomers the sources, processes, and strategies for conducting research in Oregon law. As with prior editions, librarians and other expert researchers should find the book a useful reference to Oregon legal resources and research strategies.

This edition emphasizes a user-friendly, process-oriented approach to Oregon legal research, with significant additions of checklists and summaries to provide easy, efficient access to important information. The organization of chapters follows steps in the research process but reflects recent law student and professor feedback on how readers are using this book. The first chapter focuses on the interwoven skills of research, analysis, and strategic reading. The second chapter delves into research strategies, including an introduction to researching with generative AI tools. New chapters cover local and tribal law, as these topics may be important aspects of thorough research in the state. Each chapter on primary sources integrates relevant information on updating the law. While the book continues to emphasize Westlaw and Lexis, it also explains the use of freely available sources, as they are becoming more plentiful and robust. As always, we acknowledge the permission of publishers that allow us to illustrate their products to readers.

We are grateful to Suzanne Rowe for her thorough and precise authorship for many years. Her work still permeates this edition, and her impact cannot be overstated. We are also grateful for the contributions of library colleagues to each edition, particularly Angus Nesbit, Stephanie Midkiff, Dennis Hyatt, and Jaye Barlous. Earlier editions also benefited from the contributions of Dan Barerra, Carl Bjerre, Nicole Mortemore Cartelli, Zach Conway, Jerry Curry, Elizabeth Ruiz Frost, Jessica Greathouse, Katie Green, Ryan Hall,

Megan McCombs Hays, Tim Hering, Jeff Hinman, Jennifer Hisey, Jessica Hong, Sam Jacobson, Steve Johansen, Kyung Duk Ko, Alice LaViolette, Lindsay Massara, Elayna Zammarelli Matthews, Michael Moffitt, Deborah Neighbors, Greena Ng, David Olsson, Kyra Patterson, Caulin Price, Marcus Reed, Joan Malmud Rocklin, Harvey Rogers, Lauren Russell, Layne Sawyer, Michael Schneider, David Schuman, Amy Sloan, Zachary Sykes, Donna Williamson, Ashley Wong, and Kyu Ho Youm.

Megan Austin
Kelly Reynolds
July, 2025

Series Note

The Legal Research Series published by Carolina Academic Press includes titles from many states around the country. The goal of each book is to provide law students, practitioners, paralegals, college students, and laypeople with the essential elements of legal research in each state. Unlike more bibliographic texts, the Legal Research Series books seek to explain concisely both the sources of state law research and the process for conducting legal research effectively.

Oregon Legal Research

Chapter 1

Legal Research Process, Legal Analysis, Strategic Reading

CHAPTER GOALS

After reading this chapter, you will be able to

1. List the steps of the research process;
2. Identify and explain types and weight of legal authorities;
3. Identify the fundamentals of legal analysis in each step of the research process;
4. Identify and practice strategies for reading with a professional purpose;
5. Reflect on the use of Generative Artificial Intelligence (Gen-AI) tools in the research process; and
6. Reflect on your own research process, strengths, and weaknesses.

I. Overview of Legal Research Process Steps

Legal research is challenging and complicated, so a process approach provides a good structure for learning and developing skills. As you will see in this book, the legal research process involves several research strategies that you will employ to find, analyze, and evaluate information sources. Table 1.1 lists the steps of the legal research process.

Table 1.1. Legal Research Process Steps

1. Prepare for Research
2. Find and Use Secondary Sources
3. Find and Use Federal, State, and Local Enacted Law (Constitutions, Statutes, and Ordinances)
4. Find and Use Case Law
5. Find and Use Administrative Law
6. Find and Use Legislative History
7. Update, Read, Organize, and Analyze Sources

Let's reflect on this list of research process steps. As you learn and practice legal research skills, you will realize that research is not a rigid, linear process. Often, you will start with a statute or a case if that is the information you have. You will then consult secondary sources to read some context and learn more about the relevant area of law. Also, sometimes the steps of the research process are blurred or intertwined. For example, when you find statutes, you will use the annotations to the statute to find case law or other resources; consequently, the steps of finding statutes and finding cases are not really two distinct steps but are intertwined. Another example involves updating. Professors and librarians refer to updating as a crucial step in the research process, and often discuss it as one of the final steps in your research. However, in practice, you will update your sources at many different times during your research process. For example, perhaps you found a statute that seems relevant to your problem. You may see a symbol on Lexis or Westlaw that indicates the existence of pending legislation affecting the statute. You would follow that link to look at the pending legislation. Similarly, if you are looking at the annotations to a statute and find a case that looks relevant. You would use a citator on Lexis, Westlaw, or Bloomberg to see if that case has been affected by subsequent case holdings before you spend a lot of time reading that case comprehensively and relying on it in your analysis. So, updating occurs during the research process as you find and initially evaluate sources. Even though legal research process is not rigid and linear, completing all the research steps is important because legal research is so complex. For thorough, accurate, and efficient research, you will always use legal research process steps as a structure.

II. Types and Weight of Legal Authority

When you research and analyze the law, you must keep in mind types of legal authority and the weight of legal authority. The **type** of legal authority impacts why and how you are using it. For example, you rarely cite to secondary sources in documents you file in court; but secondary sources might be one of the first types of information you research to understand a legal issue or lead you to primary authorities. Table 1.2 lists the types of legal authority. The **weight** of legal authority is important to understand because you need to know which primary sources (cases, statutes, and administrative rules) are binding on a court if the situation is litigated, and which primary sources a court is not obligated to follow but might find persuasive in deciding a matter. Table 1.3 shows the weight of legal authorities, and Table 1.4 gives an example of the types of weights of legal authorities for Oregon.

Table 1.2. Types of Legal Authority

Type	Definition	Examples
Primary	Law produced by government bodies with law-making power such as legislatures, courts, and administrative agencies.	Statutes, judicial opinions, administrative rules (regulations), and administrative decisions.
Secondary	Materials that are written about the law by attorneys, law professors, or legal editors. They analyze, discuss, and explain the law.	Treatises, law review articles, practice guides, and legal encyclopedias.

Table 1.3. Weight of Legal Authority

Mandatory Authority	Cases, statutes, and other laws that are binding on a court. The court must follow these laws.
Persuasive Authority	Laws that are not binding on a court but may be followed if relevant and well-reasoned.

Table 1.4. Example of Types and Weights of Authorities in Oregon

To answer a legal question in the State of Oregon:

Primary, Mandatory Authority (primary authorities created by a court and legislature, which are binding on an Oregon court):

1. Oregon Supreme Court decision
2. Oregon statute

Primary, Persuasive Authority (primary authorities created by a court and legislature, but not binding on an Oregon court):

1. Washington court decision
2. California statute

Secondary, Persuasive Authority (secondary authorities are never mandatory because they are not binding on a court, but they might be helpful with analysis of a legal issue).

1. Treatise or law review article, which might provide a helpful scholarly discussion of an issue.
2. Legal encyclopedia, which provides a quick overview of a topic.
3. Practice guide, which provides some checklists or forms that help with drafting your court documents.

A. Hierarchy of Primary Authority

Primary, mandatory authority exists in a hierarchy: constitutions, statutes, administrative rules, and judicial opinions. The constitution of each state is the supreme law of that state. If a statute is on point, that statute comes next in the hierarchy, followed by administrative rules. Administrative rules, issued by governmental agencies, often fill in details of a statute that has been written in more general terms. Courts write judicial opinions in litigated cases, explaining the court's reasoning in reading its decision. A judicial opinion may interpret the statute or rule, but not disregard it. A judicial opinion may, however, decide that a statute violates the constitution or that an administrative rule oversteps its bounds. If there is no constitutional rule on point, the court's opinion will be controlled by common law, also called judge-made law. The term "case law" includes judicial opinions based on the law of constitutions, statutes, and regulations, as well as those opinions based on common law.

The United States has two systems of law: federal and state. When the two overlap, such as when environmental laws are created by both Congress and the Oregon Legislature, the federal law comes above state law in the hierarchy of mandatory authority. Some areas of law are reserved for the states, and in those instances, the state law is the highest, unless it violates the federal constitution.

III. Integration of Legal Analysis and Legal Research

When you conduct legal research, you are also engaging in legal analysis. Each step of the legal research process requires you to ask yourself challenging questions and make decisions about types of sources, search terms, relevance of sources, and how the sources fit together. Table 1.5 shows the analytical process you should use in each step of the research process.

Table 1.5. Analytical Process for Each Research Step

Research Step	Analytical Process
1. Preparing to Research	framing a legal issue or multiple issues based on your client's problem and your prior knowledge; deciding on search terms that are likely to produce relevant results; selecting the proper jurisdiction for your research based on the facts and the legal issue.
2. Finding and Using Secondary Sources	questioning what type of secondary source you need to get information on your problem; questioning whether the source you found is relevant to your legal issues; articulating how the source helps you with your legal problem; questioning if you need to change or add to your search terms to find more or different sources.

3. Finding and Using Federal, State, and Local Enacted Law (Constitutions, Statutes, Ordinances)	determining if multiple statutes affect your problem; questioning if the enacted law you found is relevant to your legal issue; articulating how the statute or ordinance applies to your legal problem; questioning if key terms are defined in the statute or ordinance; questioning if you need to change or add to your search terms to find more or different sources.
4. Finding and Using Case Law	questioning if, and how, the case applies to your legal issue; deciding which facts are significant in the decision; articulating how the court's reasoning applies to your legal problem; determining how the case fits with other cases you have found; questioning if you need to change or add to your search terms to find more or different sources.
5. Finding and Using Administrative Law	deciding if administrative regulations interpret, enforce, or administer a relevant statute; articulating how administrative decisions and regulations relate to other relevant legal sources; questioning if you need to change or add to your search terms to find more or different sources.
6. Finding and Using Legislative History	deciding if you need to look for legislative history to help define a term in a statute; deciding if the legal issue or problem requires you to investigate legislative intent; questioning if you need to change or add to your search terms to find more or different sources.
7. Updating, Reading, Organizing, and Analyzing Sources	questioning if there are gaps in your research that require further research; determining how all the sources you found fit together; questioning if you need to change or add to your search terms to find more or different sources.

IV. Strategic Reading As Part of Legal Research and Analysis

When you find an information source, you need to read it to decide if it's relevant, how it applies to your problem, and how it fits into your analysis of the problem. Research studies on effective reading in law school have revealed that (1) legal reading is significantly different from other types of reading; and (2) students who read with a professional purpose and use critical reading strategies read more effectively and have higher grades. Table 1.6 explains these reading strategies.

Table 1.6. Strategies for Reading with Professional Purpose

Prior to reading:

- Find a setting that is comfortable and free of distractions
- Define and connect with your professional purpose
- Establish the context of the case: note the date of the case; consider the social and procedural context; note the identity of the parties
- Articulate how the case connects to your preexisting knowledge

During reading:

- Read all the headings and other structural aspects of the case (i.e., the first sentence of each paragraph) before you read the case carefully
- Comprehend the facts
- Predict what you will learn from the case
- Think about what questions will be answered
- Develop new questions as you are reading
- Create graphic depictions of ideas, topics, and subtopics
- Annotate the case with your questions and observations
- Paraphrase what you are reading
- Look up terms and solve confusions before you move on in your reading
- Identify the main ideas in the issue, holding, and court's reasoning
- Identify the legal rules

After reading:

- Evaluate the court's reasoning
- Brief the case
- Ask yourself questions
- Ask questions to others (professors, colleagues)
- Connect the case to your existing knowledge and experiences
- Determine how the case fits with other cases and write a synthesis

A. Legal Reading Is Different

In undergraduate courses or in non-law graduate programs, students read texts, articles, and other materials to gain an understanding of a subject. The authors of those texts write to present and explain information, so the reader understands the topic.

In contrast, in legal sources such as cases, statutes, and regulations, the author's primary purpose is not explaining or describing information to the reader. In cases, judges are issuing a legal ruling by applying law to a set of facts and listing the reasons for a particular decision. Legislators draft a law using negotiated language that often has a particular meaning with the purpose of guiding behavior. In reading legal authorities, law students are trying to **solve a legal problem** based on applying legal rules to a client's particular facts. Furthermore, legal authorities contain unfamiliar terminology. Therefore, a successful legal reader needs to read critically and reflectively, and with professional purpose.

B. Reading with Professional Purpose

Reading with professional purpose requires law students and legal professionals to actively assume the role of a lawyer representing a client, or a judge deciding a legal issue.

As a lawyer advocating for a client, you would examine and give meaning to the case based on your representation of a client: What is happening procedurally? Who are the parties? How does the case relate to others with similar issues? Is the court addressing the precise legal issue that you are investigating? How do the case facts relate to your client's situation? What are the specific arguments made by the parties in the case, and could you make those arguments in your client's situation?

As a judge reading a case, you are examining the case in the context of deciding how the law applies to the facts before you: What is the procedural posture of the case? Who are the parties? What are the applicable rules? Does the case affect the decision you will render? How does the case affect your decision?

When you adopt one of these roles in your reading, you are becoming an active, critical, and reflective reader by asking yourself questions, challenging the text, reflecting on the information, and thinking about the parts of the case strategically.

V. Reflection As Part of Legal Research Process

Often, we do not take the time to reflect on a project or assignment that we have completed, or that we are in the process of completing. However, reflecting on the research and analysis that you have done increases your metacognitive skills, identifies strengths and weaknesses in your process and results, and will eventually help increase your efficiency.

First, reflect on the research process you have used previously: What steps do you follow? What methods do you use to find secondary sources, statutes, and cases? How do you record and organize your research results? At the end of your research, do you feel confident that you have found all the sources you need? What are your research strengths? What are your research weaknesses? How do you decide that you are finished researching?

Take the answers to those questions and think about what you can do differently the next time you research to increase your confidence and address the areas that you feel are weak. Think about using multiple method of searching for primary and secondary sources, instead of just conducting a natural language search.

After each research session, or after you complete a project, reflect on the tasks that required the most time or frustrated you. Think about what you gained from that investment of time and effort. Your awareness of what you are doing during research will help you to become more thorough and efficient.

VI. Using Generative AI In Legal Research

A recent addition to the legal research landscape is the surge of generative AI tools. Throughout this book, you will see suggestions for, and discussions of, the use of Gen-AI tools in the context of research strategies. Many attorneys are using Gen-AI tools in their workflows to help with administrative tasks, brainstorm ideas for researching and drafting, summarize cases or statutes or other legal documents, organize and outline information, and create timelines and agendas for tasks. Generative AI is one more tool you have at your fingertips to help with your legal work; however, it is not a replacement for your own critical thinking skills or well-developed research strategies. As you read this book, and practice research skills, think about the most effective, efficient, and ethical ways to use Gen-AI tools as another strategy in addition to strong foundational research skills.

Chapter 2

Research Strategies

CHAPTER GOALS

After reading this chapter, you will be able to

1. Explain and implement effective research strategies;
2. Analyze and plan your research;
3. Explain the organization of legal information;
4. Effectively use multiple online research strategies;
5. Find and use print resources; and
6. Develop methods and tools for tracking and organizing your research.

As discussed in Chapter 1, every step of legal research involves analysis and strategic thinking. Even though librarians and professors talk about research process steps, you rarely will complete those steps in a linear way. Rather, the successful legal researcher will complete *all* the steps in an *analytical and strategic way*. One of the most important strategies for legal research is to invest time and effort in preparing and planning your research. Planning and preparing for research require you to understand how legal information is organized so you can decide which sources you will need to find.

Finding the sources you need requires you to use numerous online search strategies. Importantly, successful researchers use multiple strategies, rather than simply relying on one approach to locating legal information. Also, even though most of your research now relies on online resources, you still need to be able to navigate print resources for information that might not be online. Finally, effective searching for and locating legal information will not be useful if you fail to implement effective strategies for tracking and organizing research results. Ultimately, research is intertwined with analysis of the information and communication of the information to colleagues or courts. So, effective ways of keeping track of your research and organizing it in a logical way are skills crucial to professional practice. Table 2.1 gives an overview of research strategies.

Table 2.1. Overview of Research Strategies

1. Planning Strategies
2. Searching Strategies
3. Tracking and Organizing Strategies

I. Preparing and Planning Your Research

Invest time in planning your research before you start searching. Table 2.2 provides a summary of planning and preparation steps.

Table 2.2. Research Preparation and Planning

Preparation and Planning Steps	Strategies
Gather facts about the client's situation	Interview the client Review documents Talk to colleagues
Determine the client's legal issue(s)	Determine what goal(s) the client is trying to achieve Articulate legal questions that will allow the client to achieve the goal
Decide which jurisdiction's law controls	Think about whether the issues or questions involve tribal law, local law, federal law, state law, international or foreign law Think about whether multiple jurisdictions are involved
Generate a list of research terms	Ask who, what, where, when, why, and how Think about terms related to facts Think about terms related to legal principles Use a legal dictionary or thesaurus Think about synonyms

II. Understanding the Organization of Legal Information

The goal of legal research is to find all the mandatory, primary authority applicable to your legal issue or problem. With the increase of online legal information and powerful search engines, legal researchers can access sources with a few simple search terms, without necessarily encountering any organizational structure. For example, if you are researching an issue having to do with Driving Under the Influence of Intoxicants in Oregon, you can enter some very basic search terms in a browser and you will get a link that leads you to a statute on a website. The links do not provide you with any information about where the statute appears within an official code of laws, or perhaps even the date it was passed by a legislature or published. The ease of searching and the accessibility of so much legal information is convenient but might obstruct a more comprehensive view of all the legal authority that you need to find. Sources and finding tools are structured and organized to help you achieve thorough and efficient research. Understanding the basic organizational structures of legal information will help you effectively plan your research.

Legal information is organized topically and chronologically. Table 2.3 shows examples of the organization of legal information.

Table 2.3. Organization of Legal Information

Type of Organizational Structure	Examples
Topical	Statutes organized by topic into a Code (*Oregon Revised Statutes*) Regulations organized by topic into a Code (Oregon Administrative Rules) Case law organized by topic into Westlaw's Topic and Key Number system and Lexis' Topic system
Chronological	*Oregon Laws* (laws published by legislative session in date order before they are codified) Case law published in reporters in date order (reflected in the citations used for cases)

III. Online Research Sources

We search online for almost every type of information. When we are trying to find information, we are looking for the most reliable and current sites that contain official and first-hand information. As an analogy, if we are interested in eating at a certain restaurant and need to find the restaurant's hours, menu, location, daily specials, and events, we search for the restaurant's official website so we can be sure the information is up-to-date and comes from the people who have the most accurate knowledge. Once we find the restaurant's website, we look for navigation tools to find the information we need: a menu link, a contact link, a map, a list of hours. Similarly, with legal information, we want the most current, accurate, and official information. Therefore, we need to know the reliable providers of legal information and the strategies for navigating the information on the providers' platforms. Table 2.4 details online legal research providers.

Table 2.4. Online Research Providers

Commercial Providers	• Westlaw • Lexis • Bloomberg • Fastcase (Free for Oregon Bar member)
Free Providers	• Google Scholar • Social Sciences Research Network • Open Access Journals
Government Websites	• Oregon.gov • Oregon Legislature's website • Oregon Secretary of State's website • Government Printing Office website • Administrative Agency websites
Library and Repository Websites	• University and Law School Library websites (University Lewis and Clark, University of Oregon, Willamette University) • State of Oregon Law Library • Law School Institutional Repositories in Digital Commons • National Indian Law Library

Gateway Sites	• Legal Information Institute (Cornell Law School) • Findlaw • Case Law Access Project • Tribal Court Clearinghouse • Tribal Law and Policy Institute • Tribal Law Gateway (National Indian Law Library)

A. Commercial Providers

Lexis and Westlaw are the largest commercial providers of computerized legal research. They provide extensive coverage of primary and secondary authority. Both providers have reputations for accurate material and user-friendly search techniques. They run searches that are easy to construct and provide tools for narrowing to the most relevant documents. Other commercial providers of legal materials online include Bloomberg and Fastcase. Bloomberg is most often helpful in researching issues related to finance and business or in obtaining court documents. Currently, Fastcase is available to members of the Oregon State Bar for free; it provides primary authority, secondary materials, and a basic search engine. Also from the Oregon State Bar are Bar Books, practice manuals that explain legal topics and provide citations to primary sources.

B. Free Providers

One of the best free online sources for cases and law review articles is Google Scholar. It is user friendly and searching it can produce good results. The greatest weakness of this source is that it contains only cases and law review articles, not statutes, administrative rules, or other important legal materials.

A good source for law review articles, especially those that have not been published yet, is the Legal Scholarship Network on SSRN (formerly called the Social Science Research Network). Registration is free, and the most recent articles on SSRN.com often present the most cutting-edge commentary. Often, articles refer to relevant statutes and cases, providing an early boost to any research project. Also, you now have more options for Open Access Journals. By looking at a Directory of Open Access Journals (https://doaj.org), you can search for journals and articles by subject or title.

C. Government Websites

Most states and the federal government provide an abundance of legal material online for free. The main limitation to these sites is that material may be available only for a certain date range. Like most states, Oregon maintains its own websites for its primary authority, such as the Oregon Legislature's website, https://www.oregonlegislature.gov. Although print versions are the official authority, the online versions are most often used for research. In a rare instance of conflict, the official version would control.

D. Library and Repository Websites

University and law school libraries can be rich sources of free, reliable legal information. The law libraries of the three law schools in Oregon — Lewis & Clark, University of Oregon, and Willamette University — provide helpful material for researching Oregon sources. From each library's home page, look for a link to "Research" or "Research Guides."

Sometimes an academic library or public law library provides on-site patrons with access to online services for free, such as academic versions of Lexis and Westlaw products. Another very valuable site sometimes provided to library patrons is HeinOnline, with extensive coverage of federal documents and law review articles. The State of Oregon Law Library also provides access to HeinOnline.

Recently, academic institutions have been expanding their repositories to provide free access to scholarly work. For example, you can find a list of law school repositories on a platform called *bepress*.[1]

E. Gateway Sites

Some libraries contain links to sites with legal material, even when the library itself does not maintain the material. One example is Cornell Law School's "Legal Information Institute" at www.law.cornell.edu. The Oregon segments of those websites have links to Oregon cases, statutes, administrative materials, and more. A similar gateway site is FindLaw at www.findlaw.com.

---

1. https://bepress.com/categories_wdc/law-schools/.

IV. Criteria for Selecting Sources for Legal Research

To select among available online resources, remember that your goal is to find all relevant material and to ensure that the material is both accurate and authoritative. Consider the following criteria when conducting legal research online. To learn what information the resource covers and the dates of coverage, also known as the *scope* of the resource, look for a "+" or "i" or "?" icon near the top of the search screen or next to the name of a database.

Authoritative. Documents written by courts, legislatures, and administrative agencies are authoritative in that they are "the law." Articles and treatises written by recognized experts in a field are not binding, but they can be very persuasive.

Official. Look for a note on government websites indicating whether its contents are official. Often, the print versions of statutes are the official versions, while increasingly a government's online version of administrative rules will be official.

Comprehensive. Much recent material is available on many websites, but some historical material and some important secondary materials may be available only on limited websites or in print.

Contextual. Increasingly, online sources provide a table of contents and other tools that provide context for the reading. These sources are valuable because they aid understanding.

Annotated. While many sites will provide the text of a case or statute, the more helpful research sites will also provide *annotations* or links to related materials.

Current. Check both to see how recent the available material is and to ensure that the online source covers the period relevant to your research (especially when doing historical work). Some online sources are no more current than their print counterparts, and websites may contain outdated material.

Cost Effective. Online sources provided by governments and universities are free and highly reliable. When cost is an issue, consider using these sources first. Online commercial services, on the other hand, can be very expensive. Check the billing practices in your office before using commercial online sources. Also, be sure you know your office's policy regarding the printing of documents from commercial service websites, which might carry extra charges.

V. Search Strategies

There are different ways to search for legal authorities. Table 2.5 provides a checklist for the various search strategies.

Table 2.5. Search Strategy Checklist

Find by Citation	• ORS 813.010, an Oregon Revised Statute citation, can be typed into the Oregon Legislature's website, or a commercial platform • A case citation such as 167 Or. App. 489, which is the citation for *State v. Sampson*, can be typed into Google Scholar, or a commercial platform
Search Table of Contents	• The *Oregon Revised Statutes* has a table of contents of Chapters that you can browse to find relevant statutes • Books have tables of contents in the front that list the chapters or sections so you can easily find information
Search an Index	• *Oregon Revised Statutes* on the Oregon Legislature's website has an index of terms that will lead you to the relevant statute • Books have indexes in the back that list page numbers where your search terms can be found
Search by Topic	• Westlaw Topic and Key Number system organizes cases under topics and subtopics so you can find all the cases under that topic in a specific jurisdiction. You will also find the topics and key numbers in headnotes • Lexis's Topic system organizes cases under topics and subtopics so you can find all cases under that topic in a specific jurisdiction. You will also find the topics and subtopics listed in headnotes

Search with Natural Language	• Enter a search to a website or platform in the form of a question such as "what steps does a drug recognition expert have to follow to determine intoxication under the DUII statute?"
Search with Boolean Language	• Enter a search using terms and connectors, such as "drug recognition expert" and steps /p intoxicat! and DUII
Use Database Filters and Search Parameters	• Narrow search parameters by jurisdiction or type of source before you search • Use filters such as date, jurisdiction, topic, search term to narrow results after you search
Use Citators	• Use Keycite on Westlaw to find other sources that cite your source • Use Shepards on Lexis to find other sources that cite your source • Use "How Cited" or "Cited By" on Google Scholar to find other cases or articles that cite your case or article
Use Gen-AI Tools (Prompt Engineering)	• Use Lexis+AI, Westlaw Precision AI, ChatGPT, Bard, Claude to generate search terms, gain foundational knowledge about a topic, or brainstorm legal issues

A. Find with a Citation

When you have a citation to a case, statute, article, or other source, retrieving that document online is as simple as typing the citation into a designated box on the proper screen. To find an Oregon case, you will use the volume and page of a *reporter*, the books that publish these cases. The case *State v. Sampson* is published in volume 167 of *Oregon Reports, Court of Appeals*, beginning on page 489. Typing in *167 Or App 489* will take you to the case. You also can search for a case by party name, typing in *State v. Sampson*, but using the party name is less precise due to similarity of party names in many cases.

B. Search Tables of Contents and Indexes

A table of contents lists the major concepts of a book, statutory scheme, or other source, in the order that they appear in that source. Online, the broadest concepts often appear on the first screen, and you open to more specific subheadings by clicking on the concept or an icon next to it. Searching a table of contents provides two benefits. First, skimming a table of contents for your research terms can lead you to relevant portions of the database. Second, examining a table of contents can provide an overview or outline of an area of law.

An index, in contrast, lists concepts in a source alphabetically. Indexes exist online both for finding sources (e.g., Lexis lists all its sources alphabetically) and for finding material within a source (e.g., a statutory code may have an online index).

C. Search by Topic

Topic searching is effective when you are familiar with the general area of law involved in your client's issue, but you don't know the relevant statutes or cases. As examples, Westlaw and Lexis provide broad topics, ranging from Antitrust to Family Law to Tax. Each topic contains sub-topics that narrow to specific legal issues. Westlaw's tool is the Topic and Key Number system. Lexis's tool is the Topic system.

D. Search with Terms and Connectors (Boolean Language)

If you do not have a citation to a relevant source, use the search terms you generated (see Chapter 1 of this book) and create searches that will be most likely to lead to the documents you need. Most search engines allow you to conduct a search simply by typing in a single word. If the word is a term of art like "interpleader" or a cause of action that is less common, for example "kidnapping," this one-word search might be successful. In contrast, if the search is in a broad legal area like "jurisdiction" or "murder," you will need to add more terms to yield successful results.

You can create highly effective searches for specific terms by using Boolean connectors. These connectors tell the computer how terms should be placed in relation to one another in targeted documents, enabling you to control more accurately what the computer searches for.

To create a search query, think of the ideal document you would like to find and try to imagine where your search terms would be located in relation to each other within that document. Would they be in the same sentence? The same paragraph? On commercial providers like Lexis and Westlaw, you can find explanations of commands by clicking on a link called "Advanced Search," "Advanced," "Tips" or "Common Connectors." Table 2.6 details the most common connectors.

Table 2.6. Common Commands and Connectors

Boolean Connector	Example	Meaning
OR	drug OR intoxicant	Alternative terms
AND	drug AND alcohol	Both terms must be in results
"..."	"under the influence"	Exact phrase must be in results
(...)	driving and (drugs or alcohol)	Search inside parenthesis runs first
!	Intoxic!	Root expander for multiple forms of the term
/s	driv! /s drug	Terms in the same sentence
/p	driv! /p control	Terms in the same paragraph
/n	test /10 urinalysis	Terms within n (number of words) of the other term
+s	driv! +s cannabis	Terms in the same sentence and same order
+p	"drug recognition officer" +p protocol	Terms in the same paragraph and same order
+n	42 +5 1983	Term within n (number of words) and same order (this will cover for statute variants, e.g. 42 U.S.C. 1983, 42 United States Code Section 1983)

Using terms and connectors can make the research process both easy and effective, but initially it takes practice. Also, connectors vary by platform, so be sure to check "help," or "advanced search" links on the platform or website you are using.

E. Search with Natural Language

Natural language searching is the type used most often on Google and other general search engines. You simply type in a question or a list of words, and the computer program decides which words are critical, whether the words should appear in some proximity to one another, and how often they should appear in the document. In the previous example, the following sentence could be used as a natural language search: *What steps does a drug recognition expert have to follow to determine intoxication under the DUII statute?*

Lexis and Westlaw both produce relevant results from natural language queries. One search explores all the documents in their databases and returns hundreds of results. The next step, however, is the more difficult one for the researcher: sifting through all those documents to find the most relevant. Each platform provides tools for doing so, called "Filters." The filters differ slightly on each platform and for each type of document.

F. Use Filters and Search Parameters

A general search typed into a universal search bar could result in thousands of documents, many of which are irrelevant to your work. You can restrict the documents you have to review in three ways: (1) selecting a database; (2) setting pre-search limits from the main page; and (3) using filters after running a search.

Lexis and Westlaw allow—and services like Fastcase require—you to select a database before searching either with terms and connectors or with natural language. Selecting a database means restricting the sources that a search will review. Typical databases for Oregon research contain the following: Oregon cases; Oregon and federal cases; Oregon statutes and court rules; Oregon administrative regulations; and secondary sources, such as law journals from the three Oregon law schools. Even when not required to select a database before running a search, careful researchers often choose to do so.

Limiting the search's parameters before searching also controls the number and relevance of documents a search retrieves. Using drop-down menus or tabs, you can select a jurisdiction and sometimes a content type (e.g., primary authority, secondary sources, news) or a legal topic.

After conducting a search, you can still limit the results through the filters, usually found on the left side of the screen, such as date, jurisdiction, topic, type of source, search within results. Be sure to review filters with each search to ensure that you are using only those that you intend; sometimes filters automatically stay engaged until you change them or disengage them.

G. Use Citators

In each step of your research, you should be using citators to make sure your research is accurate and thorough. Each chapter of this book will describe the use of citators in the context of the type of source. This section provides an overview of the purposes of using citators, and explains citator services, how to use citators for updating and expanding research, and when to use citators. Table 2. 7 gives you the purpose of citators.

Table 2.7. Purposes of Using Citators

A. Updating sources for accuracy and currentness
B. Expanding research

A citator provides a list of all documents that have cited a legal authority. This list serves two fundamental purposes in research. First, by reviewing the documents listed by a citator, you can learn whether a legal authority is still "good law." If the case you are reading was reversed on appeal, the citator will list that appellate case. If the statute you found was later amended or declared unconstitutional, the citator will list the later legislation or the case. In those situations, the authority you started with is no longer the law, and you should not rely on it. Second, the citator list can expand your research. A citator will list every case that has cited the one you start with, and some of those later cases might have more relevant facts or more careful reasoning. A citator might also list secondary sources that analyze the case, statute, or regulation in a new and useful way. Reading these additional authorities can lead to additional support for your argument and might open new lines of analysis.

1. Examples of Citator Services

Westlaw's citator is called "KeyCite," while "Shepard's" is the citator available on Lexis. These are the premier online citators and the focus of this chapter, but others are available. Bloomberg provides "BCite," Fastcase uses "Cert Report," and Google Scholar has "How cited." Using any of these services to retrieve a list of citations is quite easy, often simply requiring you to click on a link, select a tab, or type in a citation. Analyzing the citator results and reading the authorities listed is the challenging—and the rewarding—part of using a citator. Even sophisticated citators like KeyCite and Shepard's are simply tools to aid you in determining whether an authority is still respected and identifying additional sources in your research process.

Together, these two goals of using a citator are sometimes called "updating." While you might spend more time using a citator to expand your research, ensuring the validity of your legal authorities is a required part of every research process. Courts expect lawyers to update authorities to ensure that the lawyers' arguments are well supported and present the current state of the law.[2]

2. *How and When to Use Citators*

Table 2.8. Checklist for Using a Citator

A. Access the citator list containing the information you need.

B. Analyze the symbols provided by the citator for each source.

C. Consider limiting the list of citing sources by jurisdiction, date, or other function.

D. Prioritize and read the citing sources. Analyze the impact, if any, these sources have on the authority you are updating.

Although citators are included in Chapter 1 as part of the seventh step of the research process, citators can be valuable at several different points:

First, always glance at a citator's overall assessment of a case, statute, or other authority as you begin to read it. If that authority has received negative treatment, explore that treatment before spending much time analyzing the authority.

Second, after reading a case thoroughly and deciding that it is important for your analysis, update it carefully to be sure that it is still good law. Read any sources that criticize, explain, or distinguish it, as those arguments might be raised against your client as well.

Third, use each relevant case to expand your research. A list of authorities that cite a case you know is relevant to your analysis might include additional

2. The Oregon Court of Appeals has noted that failing to update is "not excusable." *See McCarthy v. Oregon Freeze Dry, Inc.*, 158 Or App 654, 656 (1999).

resources that you have not uncovered through other steps in your research. Carefully review the list of citing sources to find other cases and secondary sources that discuss the same points of law as the first case. Reading these citing sources could lead to cases with clearer reasoning or with facts more similar to your client's situation.

Finally, update your key cases, statutes, and other important authorities just before you submit your final document or present your argument orally. KeyCite and Shepard's are continually publishing new information, and your leading case could have been overruled yesterday. While that situation is rare, you should inform your supervisor or the court, providing a copy of the authority that just changed your analysis. If needed, you can ask for time to revise your analysis in any document that relied on it. Table 2.8 gives you a checklist for when to use a citator service.

H. Use AI Tools

Recently, many generative AI platforms have emerged. The technology is still nascent, and information obtained through these platforms always needs to be verified, closely read, and updated. However, in the research context, generative AI platforms can be useful for brainstorming a legal issue, learning about foundational legal concepts, generating search terms, and summarizing legal sources and documents. Platforms include Lexis+AI, Westlaw CoCounsel, Westlaw Precision AI, Bard, Claude, ChatGPT, and more. One important skill that you will want to develop as you start to integrate Gen-AI tools into your research workflow is prompt engineering. Keep in mind that some Gen-AI tools on Lexis and Westlaw will have their own prompt-creation guidelines.

To create effective Gen-AI prompts for legal research, start with the RICE framework:

Role (assigning a role to the Gen-AI tool)

Instructions (assigning specific tasks for the Gen-AI tool)

Context (providing necessary background information)

Expectations (clarify desired outcomes)

Table 2.9 provides an example prompt.

Table 2.9. Example Prompt Using the RICE Framework

Role: You are an expert lawyer who specializes in Oregon DUII law.

Instructions: Please find and summarize statutes and cases about the definition of "drive" or "driving."

Context: The question is whether Client will be convicted of DUII. The facts are that Client was arrested and charged with DUII after an officer found her drunk and sleeping in the front seat of a car while parked on the side of the street. When the officer woke her up and asked her why she was parked there, she said she was waiting for her friend. The keys were in the ignition, but the engine was not running. Her BAC was .10.

Expectations: In addition to summaries of relevant Oregon statutes and cases, provide a well-reasoned answer to the legal question supported by relevant statutes and cases.

Remember that using Gen-AI tools is iterative. When you submit a prompt, you will look at the response, evaluate and verify the information, then create another prompt or clarify your instructions. Using Gen-AI tools requires you to have solid foundational research skills, so you can verify information and citations, as well as evaluate responses effectively.

Many law firms disallow Gen-AI tools for client work. In other words, while attorneys use Gen-AI for brainstorming and administrative types of tasks, they are not embracing it for tasks that require judgment, experience, and creativity in work for their clients. So, while Gen-AI can help with some research tasks, it is not yet a replacement for your strategic, analytical, and evaluative skills.

VI. Finding and Using Print Resources

Table 2.10. Overview: Strategies for Finding and Using Print Resources

1. Search the library catalog.
2. Once you locate a book, search the shelf nearby.
3. Use the table of contents and index in the book to locate information.
4. Look for updates to the book.

Because some legal resources are still available only in print, this section reviews techniques for researching with books. First, to find a relevant book in your library, use the online catalog. You can use a simple search with relevant terms, titles, or author names, or you can use an advanced form with specific fields for each of those search options. Be sure to look first for guidance on how to construct effective searches, as each library catalog is different. You might see a "Help" link on the search page, or you can ask a librarian for assistance.

The library catalog likely includes references to both print and online materials, as well as documents available in microfiche and other formats. Each will have been assigned a call number that allows you to find it within the library collection. The call number is a series of letters (e.g., KF is the abbreviation for American law) and numbers (e.g., 3700 is the subheading for environmental law) that places the book with others on the same topic. After you have located one book, scanning the shelves nearby can lead you to additional books that might be helpful.

Once you locate a book that appears relevant, browse the table of contents in the first few pages to get an overview of the book's coverage. If your book is part of a series, you might check both the table of contents for the entire series as well as the table of contents for a particular volume. If one of your research terms appears in the table of contents, turn to the portion of the book it references and read the text.

Another effective way to begin working with a book is to find the index. Usually, the index appears in the back of the book. In a multi-volume work, the index is likely to be in the first or last volumes, or in soft-cover books shelved with the series. Search the index for your research terms, follow any cross references to other index entries, and record the references to a particular portion of the book.

Some legal books are updated with *pocket parts*, which are additional pages designed to fit into a slot in the back cover of the book. If your book has a pocket part, more current information will appear there. When a pocket part becomes too large to fit inside the book, the publisher may produce a soft-cover supplement. Furthermore, with a series of books, a few soft-cover pamphlets might provide the most recent updates for the entire series. While print material is rarely as current as online sources, these pocket parts and supplements contain the most recent print information. Table 2.10 lists strategies for research using print resources.

VII. Tracking and Organizing Research Results

Legal professionals create and develop a range of tools for tracking and organizing legal sources. Tracking and organizing should take place throughout the research process rather than waiting until the end to wade through a mass of citations or notes. For example, you can create a research log, which can take many forms, and is one good way to organize your research as you are working through the research process. A log will also help you at the end of your research process when you are analyzing and synthesizing your research. Also, major research platforms, such as Lexis and Westlaw, provide some tools to help with tracking and organizing research.

A. Research Log

Research logs track research process steps, identify resources found during that process, and describe the information in those resources relevant to the legal problem. They can take the form of charts, tables, outlines, or spreadsheets. You should use a form that makes sense to you but is organized and comprehensive enough so that you can use it to easily communicate crucial research information to a colleague or supervisor.

B. Lexis and Westlaw

Lexis and Westlaw have folder systems in which to organize research results. Also, you can use several tools to highlight and annotate the sources you find on Lexis and Westlaw. While these tools are helpful for research conducted on commercial platforms, most likely you will use freely available websites and other sources outside of commercial platforms, so you will need a way to collect and organize all your research in one place.

VIII. Strategies for Analyzing and Synthesizing Sources and Authorities

As discussed in Chapter 1, legal analysis and legal research are intertwined. While you will engage in deep reading and analysis of each statute or case separately to gain understanding, your goal with legal research is to synthesize all the legal authorities to comprehend the applicable law and be able to communicate how it applies to your client's situation.

Many people choose to create a detailed outline of their analysis and synthesis of legal research results. Others may find that charts or tables help them analyze and synthesize their research. Whatever form you choose for your analysis and synthesis, you should identify the legal authority (case, statute, regulation), state the rule (elements, factors, principle), explain the rule, and describe how the rule applies to your client's situation. By clearly identifying these analytical parts, you will be able to see how the parts fit together into a synthesized body of law.

Below are some examples of charts, tables, and outlines to use as tools for organization, analysis, and synthesis.

A. Example 1: Table

Statement of Legal Issue:
Client's facts:
Jurisdiction:

Authority (case, statute, regulation)	Rule (elements, common law rule, factors)	Rule Explanation (the rule in context)	Application to client's facts and preliminary conclusion

B. Example 2: Outline

1) First issue or sub-issue: statement of legal issue
    a) Client's facts
    b) Authority 1 (statute, case, etc.)
        i) Rule
        ii) Rule explanation
        iii) Application to client's facts
        iv) Preliminary conclusion
    c) Authority 2 (statute, case, etc.)
        i) Rule
        ii) Rule explanation
        iii) Application to client's facts
        iv) Preliminary conclusion
2) Second issue or sub-issue: statement of the legal issue
    a) Client's facts
    b) Authority 1
        i) Rule
        ii) Rule explanation
        iii) Application to client's facts
        iv) Preliminary conclusion

Using tools to track, organize, analyze, and synthesize your research might seem like extra work at first. However, the time you invest in creating and using these tools will save you time and effort in the long-term. There is nothing more frustrating than remembering that you read a source that was helpful, but you did not note the title or citation and you must retrace your steps. Tracking and organizing as you research will increase accuracy, efficiency, and thoroughness.

Chapter 3

Finding and Using Secondary Sources

CHAPTER GOALS

After reading this chapter, you will be able to

1. Describe what a secondary source is;
2. Explain the reasons you use secondary sources in legal research;
3. Discuss and differentiate various types of secondary sources;
4. Evaluate the usefulness and impact of different types of secondary sources; and
5. Use multiple strategies to find secondary sources.

I. What Are Secondary Sources?

As discussed in Chapter 1, there are two types of legal authority: primary and secondary. Secondary authority consists of materials that are written about the law by judges, law professors, attorneys, legal editors, and sometimes law students. Examples include books such as treatises and practice guides, law journal articles, legal encyclopedias, practice aids, and current awareness resources. Secondary sources analyze, discuss, and explain the law. Primary sources, in contrast, consist of laws produced by legislatures, courts, and administrative agencies. Table 3.1 provides examples of each type of authorities.

Table 3.1. Examples or Primary and Secondary Authorities

Type	Definition	Examples
Primary	Law produced by government bodies with law-making power such as legislatures, courts, and administrative agencies.	Statutes, judicial opinions, administrative rules (regulations), and administrative decisions.
Secondary	Materials that are written about the law by attorneys, law professors, or legal editors. They analyze, discuss, and explain the law.	Treatises, law review articles, practice guides, and legal encyclopedias.

II. Using Secondary Sources

Lawyers use secondary sources to learn about the law and to find references to relevant primary authority. Secondary sources are especially useful in beginning a new research project in an unfamiliar area of law. If you were asked to research a property dispute between neighbors, where would you begin? What if your clients came to you with a letter from their neighbor's lawyer that asserted the neighbor owned the land through adverse possession? Wouldn't it be helpful to have a simple explanation of the term "adverse possession" as well as an overview of its elements? And to have summaries of key statutes and cases about adverse possession? Even to have samples of the documents you might use in litigation about the ownership of the property? Secondary sources can provide you with all of that.

Secondary sources vary in how persuasive they are to courts. Common secondary sources that can be highly regarded by courts include treatises and law review articles. Also under the large umbrella of secondary sources are tools called "practice aids"; they carry no persuasive value but assist lawyers in conducting research, creating documents, and staying current in legal developments. Examples of practice aids include legal forms, jury instructions, pleadings, briefs, and blogs. All these sources are "secondary" because they are written by law professors, practicing attorneys, legal editors, and even law students.

Despite the value of secondary sources, rarely will you cite a secondary source in writing a memorandum or brief. Even sources that carry some authority, including law review articles and treatises, should be cited infrequently. By citing secondary sources, you are admitting to your reader that you could not find any primary authority supporting your arguments, thereby weakening those arguments substantially.

Three exceptions exist. First, sometimes you need to summarize the development of the law. If no case has provided a summary, citing a treatise or law review article that traces that development could be helpful to your reader. Next, citation to a secondary source is appropriate when there is no law on point for an argument you are making, which may occur with new issues or when you are arguing to expand or change the law. In these situations, your only support might come from a law review article. Finally, a secondary source may provide additional support for a point for which a primary authority already has been cited. For example, you can bolster an argument supported by a case, especially if it is from another jurisdiction, by also citing an article or treatise by a respected expert on the topic.

III. Evaluating Secondary Sources

Even if you do not cite a secondary source in a document, you must decide the weight to give the source in developing your own analysis. Consider the following criteria:

- ***Who is the author?*** The views of a respected scholar, an acknowledged expert, or a judge carry more weight than a student author or an anonymous editor.
- ***When was the material published?*** Especially for cutting-edge issues, a more recent article is likely to be more helpful. Even with more traditional issues, be sure that the material analyzes the current state of the law.
- ***Where was the material published?*** Treatises from leading publishers will always be more authoritative than an opinion expressed on a blog. For law review articles, those published in established law journals are generally granted the most respect. A school's prestige and the length of the journal's existence can influence how well established a journal is. Thus, a journal that has been published for a century at a top law school may carry more respect than a new journal at an unaccredited school. A publication specific to your jurisdiction or dedicated to a particular topic, however, could be more helpful than a publication from another state or one with a general focus.

- ***What depth is provided?*** The more focused and thorough the analysis, the more useful the material will be.
- ***How relevant is it to your argument?*** If the author is arguing your exact point, the material will be more persuasive than if the author's arguments are only tangential to yours.
- ***Has this secondary source been cited previously by courts?*** If a court has found a source persuasive in the past, it is likely to find it persuasive again. Remember that the text of a secondary source may become primary authority if it is adopted by a court or legislature.
- ***What is the scope of the source?*** The source covers certain types of information. Consider that another source might have more relevant information for your particular inquiry.

IV. Types of Secondary Sources

Table 3.2. Examples of Secondary Sources and Their Use

Secondary Source Type	Examples of Use
Legal Encyclopedias	Brief, general overview of a legal topic
Treatises	In-depth, comprehensive knowledge of an area of law; citations to primary law
Practice Guides (Oregon Bar Books)	Practical outline and overview of a legal topic; citations to primary law.
Law Journal Articles	Deep analysis of a narrow topic; advocacy for legal change; citations to primary law
Practice Aids (jury instructions, forms, briefs and pleadings, dockets, etc.)	Prepare and draft court documents
American Law Reports Annotations	Multi-jurisdictional overview of narrow topic; citations to primary law
Government Websites	Regulatory information, news, FAQs, practical tools
Blogs	Current topics, legal news

Different research projects will benefit from different secondary sources. For a broad overview of an area of law, especially at the beginning of a project, an encyclopedia may be best. For in-depth analysis on a narrow topic, a law review article is more likely to be helpful. On cutting-edge issues, articles from SSRN, legal news databases, and blogs will cover new areas of law quickly. In litigation, court-approved forms and uniform jury instructions will be indispensable. Table 3.2 gives examples of different types of secondary sources.

Consider your own background in the subject matter and the goals of your research and select from these sources accordingly. A source that was not helpful in your last research project may be perfect for the current project. How many secondary sources you use depends on the success of your early searches and the time available to you.

A. Legal Encyclopedia

Legal encyclopedias summarize information on a wide variety of legal subjects. They are organized by subject matter according to topics selected by the publisher. These topics are presented alphabetically, both in an online table of contents or in bound volumes. The two national legal encyclopedias are *Corpus Juris Secundum* (CJS) and *American Jurisprudence, Second Edition* (Am Jur 2d). Some larger states have their own encyclopedias, such as *California Jurisprudence* and *Florida Jurisprudence*. Oregon does not have its own encyclopedia.

One potentially helpful feature of an encyclopedia is the list of footnotes accompanying the text. If a footnote refers to recent primary authority from your jurisdiction, you will have made a great step forward in your research. However, because the footnotes in CJS and Am Jur 2d cite to authorities from all American jurisdictions and tend to be dated, you will need to use those citations as a springboard to recent Oregon materials.

An encyclopedia may also contain cross references to other sources. For example, CJS includes cross references to *American Law Reports*, a secondary source discussed later in this chapter and to West's Key Number Digest that indexes cases by topic. Table 3.3 lists where to find legal encyclopedia.

Table 3.3. Where to Find Legal Encyclopedia

Examples	Where to Find
1. American Jurisprudence	Westlaw, Lexis
2. Corpus Juris Secundum	Westlaw
3. Wex	Legal Information Institute

Often, you will choose an encyclopedia at the beginning of your research, especially if you are unfamiliar with a basic term or concept. For example, perhaps a client calls and asks about the rules for "rest periods" at work. You might choose to use Am Jur 2d on Westlaw to become familiar with the requirements of rest periods.

- Set search parameters: On Westlaw, you would select the secondary sources database and then select the encyclopedias and jurisprudence link.
- Use a Boolean search: Then in the search box, enter a "terms and connectors" search such as *employment and "rest period."*
- Use filters to narrow results: On the left side, use the publication name filter to select Am Jur 2d.

If you are using a free encyclopedia, Wex from the Legal Information Institute, you will find that it provides limited coverage, with entries covering legal terminology rather than broader concepts. For example, if you are trying to find basic information about at-will employment, you can

- Browse the entries on Wex alphabetically, or
- Enter search terms such as *at-will employment* in the search box, and
- Use filters on the left side to narrow results.

An encyclopedia will provide an overview of a topic or term and refer you to more information sources such as cases, statutes, or law journal articles, so it is a good entry point into further research.

B. Books

Table 3.4. Where to Find Books

Type	Examples	Where to Find
Treatises	*Oregon Evidence*	Lexis
	Oregon Law and Practice	Westlaw
	Federal Evidence	Law Library and Westlaw
Hornbooks	*Fletcher, Federal Indian Law*	West Academic Study Aids and Law Library
	Dobbs, Hornbook on Torts	West Academic Study Aids and Law Library
Practice Guides	*Oregon Bar Books*	Oregon State Bar and Lexis
	Practising Law Institute Series	HeinOnline, ABA
Nutshells	*Trial and Lawyering Skills in a Nutshell*	West Academic Study Aids and Law Library

A book on a legal topic provides an in-depth discussion of the topic and relevant references to primary authority. Legal texts include treatises, hornbooks, practice guides, and *Nutshells*. These books have the same purpose: to cover a particular legal subject, such as contracts or civil procedure. They are distinguished mainly by their level of coverage.

- Treatises offer comprehensive coverage of a subject. Some are very academic and sophisticated in their approach, but many are very accessible. Attorneys often begin work on unfamiliar areas of law with treatises.
- Hornbooks offer a slightly more summarized view of legal subjects. They can be as lengthy as treatises but are targeted to students and other novices.
- Practice guides typically cover an area of law thoroughly, but with a particular focus on the nuts and bolts of practice as opposed to the more theoretical approach of treatises or hornbooks. A practice guide is likely to include explanations (e.g., the elements of a cause of action), references to primary authority, sample forms, and practice tips.
- *Nutshells* are a series of small books published by West that offer condensed explanations of law.

Table 3.4 lists where to find various types of books.

1. Treatises

Treatises specific to Oregon law are limited. *Oregon Evidence* and *Oregon Law and Practice: Civil Procedure* are two treatises on Oregon law that are easily accessible. But even a general treatise with a national scope can provide useful background information to launch a research project.

The authoritative value of a treatise depends largely on the reputation of the author. Professor Laird Kirkpatrick, for example, is a widely recognized expert on Oregon evidence, and his one-volume treatise is so respected that it is cited by courts. A widely used treatise on practice in federal courts is Wright & Miller's *Federal Practice and Procedure*, a multi-volume treatise.

Research strategies for treatises: During the representation of a client, you might need to investigate a topic or issue more comprehensively. For example, you have a question about expert testimony in Oregon and want to access a comprehensive discussion of that topic. You decide to use Lexis to find a treatise:

- Set search parameters: On Lexis, choose the secondary sources database, then select Treatises and Guides. Then scroll down to the State options and choose Oregon.
- Browse the list of publications by title to find Oregon Evidence. Or enter a search in the search box.
- Browse the table of contents of Oregon Evidence, or search in the book with search terms.

Law libraries provide access to treatises in print, as well as some e-book options. For example, public law libraries, such as the State of Oregon Law Library, allow all Oregon residents to set up accounts to access Legal Information Resource Center publications.

2. Practice Guides

One of the most helpful secondary sources for Oregon attorneys is the series of practice guides published by the Oregon State Bar (OSB), known as BarBooks. Each guide covers one area of Oregon law in depth. Titles address administrative law, construction law, environmental law, family and juvenile law, real property, torts, and trial practice, among many other areas of Oregon law. The authors are typically practitioners with extensive experience in the legal area they are writing about. The text is practice-oriented, so it includes explanations, references to primary authority, practice tips, and sample forms.

BarBooks are available for download from the OSB website; they are free to bar members and to other users and libraries with subscription access. In print, BarBooks are published as loose-leaf binders.

In addition to the OSB series, West's Oregon Law and Practice series addresses a few topics of Oregon law in a similar manner. In that series, the Civil Procedure title is available on Westlaw. Some libraries have all the series titles in print.

More general practice guides are published by the Practising Law Institute (PLI), the American Law Institute (ALI), and the American Bar Association (ABA). If you can't find a state-specific guide, you might try a general practice guide.

Research strategies for practice guides: Use a practice guide to find succinct explanations of Oregon law and citations to relevant statutes and cases. For example, on the issue of rest periods at work, you might have learned some basic information from the encyclopedia, but now you want a more specific explanation of Oregon law with references to primary sources. You decide to look at Oregon Bar Books.

- From the Oregon BarBooks platform, browse the list of titles or enter a search into the "document text" search bar.
- Use Filters on the left side to narrow your search if necessary.
- Select a result from the results list. In addition to reading the particular section that came up in your results, use the Table of Contents link in the upper left side of the page to read additional sections if necessary.

C. Law Reviews and Journals

Table 3.5. Oregon Law Reviews and Journals

Examples of Oregon Law Reviews and Journals	Where to Find
Environmental Law Review Oregon Law Review Journal of Environmental Law and Litigation Oregon Review of International Law Animal Law Review Willamette Journal of Social Justice and Equity Willamette Sports Law Journal Lewis & Clark Law Review	HeinOnline, Westlaw, Lexis, Google Scholar, Institutional Repositories

Law reviews and law journals publish scholarly articles written by law professors, judges, practitioners, and students. Each article addresses in detail a specific legal issue. Freed from the constraints of representing a client's interests or deciding a particular case, an author can explore whether the laws currently in force are the best legal rules and to propose changes.

Reading articles published in law reviews and journals can provide a thorough understanding of current law because the authors often explain the existing law before making their recommendations. These articles also may identify weaknesses or new trends in the law that might address your client's situation. Sometimes an article compares laws in different jurisdictions, pointing out the benefits or problems in each. The footnotes in law review and law journal articles can provide excellent summaries of relevant research. Table 3.5 shows the various Oregon law reviews and journals.

Articles written by students are called "Notes" or "Comments." Although not as authoritative as articles written by recognized experts, student articles can provide clear and careful analysis and their footnotes can contain valuable research leads. Shorter law review pieces, generally written by students, simply summarize a recent case that the publication's editors consider important. These are called "Case Notes" or "Recent Developments." They notify readers of important developments in the law, but do not analyze or critique the case in any depth. They are often not helpful beyond offering a short summary of the case and the court's analysis.

Research strategies for law reviews and journals: To research a particular issue in depth, you might use several strategies.

- If you have found and read a particular statute or case relevant to your issue and want to read more about the issue, you could use a citator, Shepard's on Lexis or Key Cite on Westlaw, to find a law review or journal article that cites to that law.
- If you are unfamiliar with a legal issue and want to do background reading, you would use a database such as the law journal library on HeinOnline or narrow your search parameters on Lexis or Westlaw to search only law reviews and journals and enter search terms.
- Go to the Legal Scholarship Network (SSRN) or an institutional repository and do an advanced search or browse by subject area.

D. Practice Materials

You can choose from a variety of practice materials to brainstorm ideas for researching a legal topic, to find primary sources, and to see examples of various types of legal documents. Some common practice materials are forms, jury instructions, briefs and pleadings, and court dockets. Table 3.6 shows where to find common practice materials.

Table 3.6. Common Practice Materials

Type of Resource	Examples	Where to Find
Forms	Oregon Statutory Forms Criminal Law Formbook	*Oregon Revised Statutes* Court websites Westlaw Lexis
Jury Instructions	Oregon Criminal Jury Instructions Oregon Civil Jury Instructions	Oregon BarBooks Westlaw Lexis
Briefs and Pleadings	Complaints, Petitions, Answers, Memoranda of Law, Motions	Westlaw Lexis Court websites
Dockets	Oregon court dockets	Oregon Judicial Case Information Network (OJCIN), Lexis (Courtlink), Westlaw
	Federal court dockets	Lexis (Courtlink), Westlaw Bloomberg, PACER

1. Forms

A form can be a great shortcut in drafting a legal document, especially a document you are drafting for the first time in an unfamiliar area of law. Forms are available in a diverse range of sources. When using forms, be aware that they are designed for general audiences, not your client or situation. Before using a form, ensure that you understand every word in the form and modify it to suit your needs. Do not simply fill in the blanks and assume that the form correctly represents your client's position or your situation. Unless a particular form is prescribed by statute or by a court, revise the wording to avoid unnecessary legalese.

Research strategies for forms:

- *Oregon Revised Statutes*: The ORS provides forms for some situations. To give two examples, ORS 127.531 contains a form for an advance directive concerning health care and ORS 100.740 contains language that must be included in a condominium sales agreement. To find statutory forms, search the ORS General Index on the Oregon Legislature's website under "Forms (Statutory)."
- Lexis or Westlaw: On Westlaw, you can go to the *Oregon Revised Statutes* and look on the right side of the screen for "Index — Oregon Statutes" and use the alphabetical navigation to find forms. For a full-text search, use terms for the substantive content and the term "form" (e.g., *advance directive form*). Also, Westlaw has a link to "Oregon Form Finder" under the "State Materials" tab and "Oregon" link. Lexis provides access to Matthew Bender Oregon Forms.
- Formbooks and practice guides: A "formbook" may provide actual forms or suggested language that you can use in crafting your document. Examples of Oregon formbooks include *Criminal Law Formbook* and *Administering Oregon Estates*. Federal forms are available in numerous titles, including *West's Federal Forms* and *American Jurisprudence Legal Forms 2d*. Search the library catalog by subject for topical formbooks.
- Oregon Court websites: The site has a variety of forms related to family law, stalking orders, name change, and other subjects. The websites of circuit courts in Oregon may contain more forms.
- Oregon State Bar website: the Oregon State Bar website provides a "Forms Library" for forms related to admission to practice law.
- Other commercial sources: Gale's Legal Forms Library includes forms ranging from business transactions to wills. Contents include forms required by a state entity (i.e., "official forms"), forms drawn from public records, forms drafted by firms for use in a particular state, and generic forms. Check your library to see whether it has a Gale subscription for Oregon forms. If not, you might also try the general form service provided by Gale for a modest fee: U.S. Legal Forms. An additional commercial source is Stevens-Ness Law Publishing. When searching one of these sites, look for links to "Legal Forms," and, if possible, search by "Oregon" for state-specific forms. The State of Oregon Law Library also provides access to forms.

2. Jury Instructions and Verdicts

At the close of a trial, the judge instructs the jury before it begins to deliberate. These instructions outline the law; in other words, they tell a lawyer preparing for trial what she must prove to prevail. By examining the instructions in advance of trial, an attorney may be better able to present evidence to the jury. Even if a case ends before trial, knowing the instructions a jury would receive may produce more effective research. The Oregon State Bar has committees on uniform jury instructions for both civil and criminal matters.

Another useful piece of information for the lawyer preparing for trial — or hoping to settle a case — is the dollar amount of verdicts or settlements in similar cases in the past. A subscription service called "Jury Verdicts Northwest" provides this information in print and online.

Research strategies for jury instructions:

- Oregon BarBooks: The *Uniform Civil Jury Instructions* and *Uniform Criminal Jury Instructions* are available by browsing or searching on the BarBooks platform. They are also available in print, in loose-leaf binders.
- Lexis and Westlaw: On Lexis, in the main search bar, start typing Oregon Uniform Criminal (or Civil) Jury Instructions, and the search will autofill. You also can select the secondary sources database from the Content menu and browse titles. You can browse the table of contents, or search within the source. On Westlaw, select secondary sources, then scroll down to "By Type" and select Oregon. Oregon Uniform Criminal Jury Instructions and Oregon Uniform Civil Jury Instructions are listed in the sources.

3. Briefs and Pleadings

Court documents such as briefs, pleadings (complaints, petitions, answers, declarations, and memoranda), and motions are useful practical guides when you are researching or drafting your own court documents.

Research strategies for briefs and pleadings:

- Use a citator: On Lexis or Westlaw, if you are looking at a statute, case, or regulation, and you want to find a court document that cites to that particular primary law, you can use "Other Citing Sources" on Lexis and then use the filters on the left side to narrow your results to Briefs, Motions, or Pleadings. Similarly, on Westlaw, use "Citing References," then choose "Trial Court Documents" then filter to the type of document you are interested in.

- Set search parameters: On Lexis, from Content, select "Briefs, Pleadings & Motions" and conduct a Boolean or natural language search or you can limit your search by type, jurisdiction, or practice area before entering a search. On Westlaw, from Content Types, select Briefs or Trial Court Documents and conduct a Boolean or natural language search, or you can limit your search by type, jurisdiction, or topic before entering a search.
- Boolean or natural language search: On Lexis or Westlaw, on the main start page, enter your Boolean or natural language search in the search bar, then use the filters on the left side to limit your results to Briefs, Pleadings, Motions, or Trial Court Documents.

4. Dockets

Dockets are formal records noting all proceedings and filings in court cases. You can use dockets to follow important cases on issues that are of interest. You can also look at documents filed in those cases and use them to inform your own research.

Research strategies for dockets:

- Bloomberg: Bloomberg provides access to dockets for federal courts and a few state courts, but not Oregon state courts. You can also access and download PDFs of many of the documents filed in court. Be aware that Bloomberg limits the number of documents you can access through an academic subscription.
- Lexis: Lexis provides access to dockets through CourtLink. You can search dockets only, court documents only, or dockets and documents together. You can use filters on the left side to narrow your results. Freely available documents will be linked on the docket sheet.
- Westlaw: Westlaw has a dockets database that you can search by federal court, agency, state court, by territory, or by topic. There are docket-related tools on the right side of the screen. You can order documents that are not already online.
- PACER: Public Access to Court Electronic Records is available for access to federal court dockets and documents. There is no fee to sign up for an account; however, there is a fee to access court records once logged into PACER. If you accrue $30 or less of charges in a quarter, charges are

waived for that quarter. Some academic institutions provide access to PACER for faculty and students.

- Oregon Judicial Case Information Network (OJCIN): OJCIN provides access to Oregon court records via a paid subscription. Some academic libraries provide access to OJCIN.

E. American Law Reports

American Law Reports (ALR) is a hybrid resource, offering both commentary on certain legal subjects and the full text of published cases on those subjects. Because cases are now so widely available, researchers use ALR almost exclusively for the commentary articles. These articles tend to focus on very narrow topics, take a practitioner's view, and provide a survey of the law in different jurisdictions. An article on the exact topic of your research is likely to be extremely helpful. Commentary articles are written by lawyers who are knowledgeable but are not necessarily recognized experts. The "Table of Cases, Laws, and Rules" lists related authorities by jurisdiction, making it a powerful research tool. "Research References" include citations for related statutes, encyclopedia entries, treatises, and other sources. Tables of Contents for the articles help you understand the analytical structure of an issue or topic.

Research strategies for American Law Reports:

Lexis: Set search parameters by selecting Secondary Sources, then selecting American Law Reports from the "National" category:

- Enter a search in the search bar, or
- Use the search template to conduct a search.

Westlaw: Set search parameters by selecting Secondary Sources, then go to "Type" and select American Law Reports:

- Conduct a Boolean or natural language search in the search box, or
- Use the list of topics to narrow further before you search, or
- Use the American Law Reports Index on the right side of the screen to find an article on your topic.

Citator: In Lexis or Westlaw, if you are looking at a case or a statute and you want to read an ALR article on the topic, you can use "Other Citing Sources" on Lexis and Citing References on Westlaw and then narrow to secondary sources and then to ALR.

F. Government Websites

Table 3.7. Finding Government Websites

Examples	How to Find
Administrative Agency Websites	Google Advanced search (using .gov domain) Official website for the State of Oregon (Oregon.gov) Federal Register (for Federal Administrative Agencies) (federalregister.gov/agencies)
Legislative websites	Google Advanced search (using .gov domain)

Governmental entities such as legislatures and administrative agencies have created websites containing extensive amounts of helpful information. In addition to linking to primary sources, government agencies provide reports, FAQs, forms, tools, and other publications that help you find and understand legal principles within their jurisdiction. Table 3.7 lists how to find government websites.

Research strategies for government websites: With this wealth of information available for free, you will often find helpful secondary sources just by using a Google type of search. On Google, you can refine your searches to be more efficient by using an Advanced Search and specifying a "site or domain." For example, if you just want government sites, you can type .gov into the site or domain search box and then put other search terms in the boxes at the top of the Advanced Search page. Or, if you want to search a particular site, you can type that site name and then add search terms. This type of searching will allow you to eliminate irrelevant results and save time and energy.

G. Current Awareness Resources

Table 3.8. Where to Find Current Awareness Resources

Examples	Where to Find
Articles on cutting-edge issues	SSRN Legal Scholarship Network, *bepress* legal repository
Blogs	ABA Journal Blawg Directory
Legal News	Lexis—Law 360, National Law Journal, Westlaw—News

There are many resources to help you keep current on a particular legal topic or issue. You can often set alerts for specific types of information. For example, legal news sources and "blawgs," as law blogs are often called, can be very useful for keeping current. Many blawgs are well respected for tracking developments in case law, statutes, and regulations. They are written by attorneys and law professors with extensive experience in a practice area. Table 3.8 shows where to find various current awareness resources.

Law 360 is a legal news platform that you can access through Lexis. Other legal news publications, such as the National Law Journal, are available on the Lexis platform.

The Legal Scholarship Network on SSRN is an open access platform where authors upload their research papers in the digital library, so that scholars can access groundbreaking research and working papers. Similarly, the *bepress* Legal Repository provides access to pre-prints and working papers from legal professionals and scholars.

Research strategies for current awareness resources:

- SSRN Legal Scholarship Network: You can search by recent papers, or by topic. You can also subscribe to ejournal alerts.
- *bepress* legal repository: You can browse by institution or subject or enter search terms. You can sign up for notifications by email or RSS.
- Blogs: To select a useful law blog, you might begin with the *ABA Journal*'s top 100 blawg list. The list separates the blogs into practice

areas, making it easy to find one relevant to your work. Another useful directory of law blogs is BlawgSearch, published by Justia, which organizes thousands of law-related blogs into 75 topical areas. Lexis provides access to blogs by navigating to the News database under the Content tab. Also, you can do a Google-type search on your browser with the legal topic you are interested in and include the search term blog. For example, you could type in *civil rights blog.* Always learn more about the organization, law firm, or individual author of the blog by looking at the "About" link. Finally, you can search Law 360 by selecting a specific section first or entering search terms in the general search bar.

Chapter 4

Researching the Oregon Constitution

CHAPTER GOALS

After reading this chapter, you will be able to

1. Locate the constitution and identify relevant provisions and amendments;
2. Explain how to find sources interpreting the constitution; and
3. Describe the initiative and referendum amendments and how to find relevant materials on the amendments.

I. Overview

A constitution is the basic law of a state or nation. It creates the structure of the government, establishes processes, and defines the scope of a government's power. A constitution also sets the fundamental rights of its citizens. The U.S. Constitution is the supreme law of the country. Although state constitutions cannot conflict with the U.S. Constitution, they can provide more protections. Oregon's constitution is much longer: it has over 60,000 words while the U.S. Constitution has 7,591 words.

The Oregon Constitution is usually published with the *Oregon Revised Statutes*, and you can use indexes and other statutory finding aids to locate relevant provisions. These tools are discussed in Chapter 5. To interpret a provision of the constitution, researchers should read the text, analyze case law interpreting the provision, and look at the historical circumstances in which the constitutional provision was adopted. The constitution can be amended in two ways: (1) directly by voters through initiative or (2) by the majority of both houses of the legislature referring a change to the voters. The initiative and referral process can also be used for statutes, while the referendum can be used by voters to reject legislation.

This chapter focuses on researching the Oregon Constitution. The first section explores the framework and organization of the constitution. Next, the chapter explains how to find constitutional provisions and interpret them. Finally, it will discuss initiative and referendum research.

II. Researching the Oregon Constitution

A. Constitution Framework

The Oregon Constitution is arranged topically by articles which are divided into sections. The constitution defines the rights of the people (Article I), establishes the election process (Article II), and sets up the structure of the state government (see Table 4.1 below).

Table 4.1. Structure of Oregon State Government

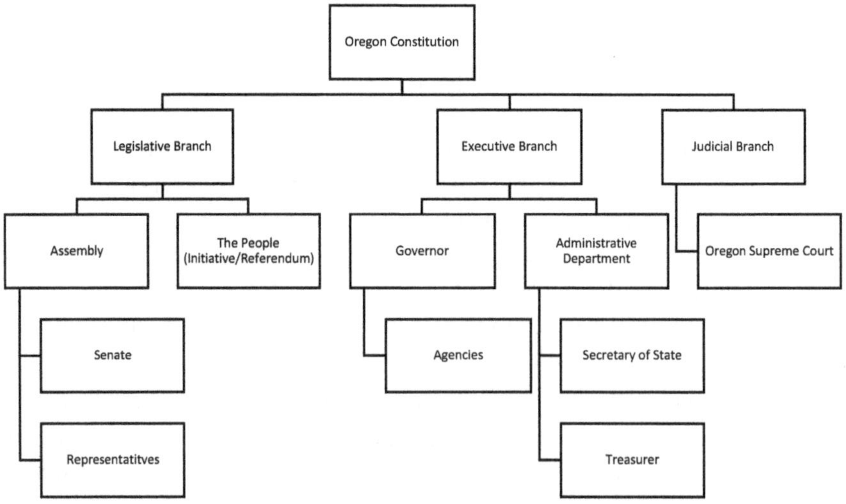

While some provisions parallel many of the familiar provisions of the U.S. Constitution, others seem much more statutory in nature. For example, Article I gives the state the power to permit the sale of liquor by the glass. Therefore, you should always check to see whether a constitutional provision affects your research problem even when that possibility seems unlikely.

B. Finding Constitution Provisions

The Oregon Constitution is typically published with the *Oregon Revised Statutes* (ORS). Finding provisions within the constitution depends on the platform or publication that you are using. The Oregon Legislature's website and the official print version of the ORS have specific indexes for the Oregon Constitution in addition to the general index. While Westlaw's general index also provides references to the constitution, Westlaw does not have a dedicated index for the Oregon Constitution. Table 4.2 lists various ways to find constitutional provisions.

Table 4.2. Ways to Find Constitutional Provisions

Publication/ Platform	Location	Finding Aids	References
Oregon Legislature's Website (free)	Bills and Laws Tab > Oregon Constitution (left frame)[1]	• Index to the Oregon Constitution (top, middle frame) • Table of Contents	ORS Annotations (left frame)
Lexis	State > Oregon > OR—LexisNexis® Oregon Annotated Constitution	• Table of Contents • Search • Index—Oregon Statutes (right frame) provides references to the constitution	• Notes to Decisions (following the text of the section) • Shepardize Document (right frame of the section)

1. https://www.oregonlegislature.gov/bills_laws/Pages/OrConst.aspx.

Westlaw	State Materials > Oregon > Statutes and Court Rules > Constitution of Oregon (listed after the statutes in the table of contents)	• Table of Contents • Search Index-Oregon Statutes (right frame) provides references to the constitution	• Notes of Decisions tab • Citing References tab • Context & Analysis tab
Oregon Revised Statutes (print)	Volume 19	• Constitution Index (located after the text of the Constitution) • ORS Index provides references to the constitution	ORS Annotations volume
West's Oregon Revised Statutes Annotated (WORSA)	End of the set	General Index provides references to the constitution	Notes of Decisions (located after the text of the section)

As with statutory research, each section of the Constitution will have references or annotations to sources that discuss that section. These sources might be cases, Attorney General opinions, and law review articles. Lexis and Westlaw will include references with the text of the section. The Oregon legislature website and the print ORS list references in a separate location: the ORS Annotations link on the website or the ORS Annotations volume at the end of the print set.[2]

2. For more information on statutory research, see Chapter 5, Enacted Law, section III.

III. Interpreting the Oregon Constitution

Interpreting the Oregon Constitution requires researchers to look closely at the text of a constitutional provision, cases that interpret that provision, and the historical circumstances surrounding its adoption. This interpretation approach was set forth by the Oregon Supreme Court in *Priest v. Pearce*, 314 Or 411, 415–16 (1992), so it is referred to as the Priest Framework.[3] This section will explore the Priest Framework and its exceptions.

A. Text and Case Law

Begin by reading the words of the constitutional provision carefully. If it is a lengthy provision, outlining it may help you understand it. Then read cases that address the provision. Reading the cases cited in those cases may provide important context.

To find cases that interpret a provision, use the tools listed in the Finding References column in the table above. The process is identical to finding cases that interpret a statute, so please refer to Chapter 5, section V for a more extensive discussion of this topic.

B. Historical Circumstances

The final step in the Priest Framework is to look at the historical circumstances in which the constitutional provision was adopted. By looking at the historical circumstances, the court is trying to decipher the intentions and understanding of the delegates to the convention, the voters, and/or the legislators. The sources consulted depend on the type of constitutional provision. Table 4.3 provides examples of these sources.

3. *See also Couey v. Atkins*, 357 Or 460, 490, 355 P3d 866 (2015).

Table 4.3. Examples of Historical Circumstances Sources

Type of Provision	Intent	Example of Sources
Original 1857 Constitution	• Intent of delegates to the convention • Intent of the voters who ratified	• The Oregon Constitution and Proceedings and Debates of the Constitutional Convention of 1857 • A Legislative History of the Oregon Constitution of 1857
Initiative	Intent of voters	• Official Voter's Pamphlet • Press accounts, newspaper and magazine editorials
Referral	Intent of legislators	• Legislative history
	Intent of voters	• Official Voter's Pamphlet • Press accounts, newspaper and magazine editorials

1. Original 1857 Constitution

The drafters of the Oregon Constitution did not have an official reporter. The *Journal of the Constitutional Convention* contains only a record of the official actions of the delegates, so it is of limited value. In 1926, Charles H. Carey combined the entries from the *Journal* with various newspaper accounts from the convention. The resulting book, *The Oregon Constitution and Proceedings and Debates of the Constitutional Convention of 1857*,[4] is an invaluable resource for understanding the historical circumstances surrounding Oregon's constitution and is cited frequently by courts.[5]

Another indispensable source for insights into the drafters' intent is Claudia Burton's three-part article series entitled *A Legislative History of the Oregon Constitution of 1857*.[6] These articles resulted from a discovery at the Oregon

4. *The Oregon Constitution and Proceedings and Debates of the Constitutional Convention of 1857* (Charles H. Carey ed., State Printing Dept. 1926).

5. Use caution when referencing the articles in this book, however, since major newspaper editors were also delegates at the convention. David Schuman, *The Creation of the Oregon Constitution*, 74 Or L Rev 611, 622 (1995).

6. Claudia Burton & Andrew Grade, *A Legislative History of the Oregon Constitution of 1857—Part I (Articles I & II)*, 37 Willamette L Rev 469 (2001); Claudia Burton,

Historical Society of a nearly intact set of documents for each article of the Oregon Constitution. Table 4.4 gives the location of these sources.

In examining the historical circumstances of Oregon's constitution, Oregon courts often look to other material as well. The Magna Carta and English legal commentators are sometimes cited. Because the drafters modeled the Oregon Constitution after the Indiana Constitution's Bill of Rights, that document has been persuasive. A chart by W.C. Palmer entitled *The Sources of the Oregon Constitution* compares sections of Oregon's constitution to the constitutions of Indiana and other states.[7] For a thorough bibliography of sources, see Appendix 1A Interpreting the Oregon Constitution: An Annotated Bibliography in the Oregon Constitutional Law Barbook.[8]

Table 4.4. Location of Sources for the 1857 Constitution

Source	Location
Journal of the Constitutional Convention	HathiTrust
The Oregon Constitution and Proceedings and Debates of the Constitutional Convention of 1857	HathiTrust
A Legislative History of the Oregon Constitution of 1857: • *Part I (Articles I & II): 37 Willamette L Rev 469* • *Part II (Articles III–VII), 39 Willamette L Rev 245* • *Part III (Articles VIII–XVIII), 40 Willamette L Rev 225*	HeinOnline

2. Amendments: Initiatives and Referrals

Researchers consult different sources to determine the historical circumstances surrounding amendments to the Oregon Constitution. As discussed in section III of this chapter, the Oregon Constitution can be amended in two ways: initiatives and referrals.

Initiatives are voter proposed petitions. Therefore, determining the historical circumstances of an initiative will involve looking at voter intent. A court

A Legislative History of the Oregon Constitution of 1857—Part II (Frame of Government: Articles III–VII), 39 Willamette L Rev 245 (2003); Claudia Burton, *A Legislative History of the Oregon Constitution of 1857—Part III* (Mostly Miscellaneous: Articles VIII–XVIII), 40 Willamette L Rev 225 (2004).

7. 5 Or L Rev 200 (1925–1926).

8. Jack L. Landau, Chapter 1: *Constitutionalism*, (OSB Legal Pubs., 2022). Oregon Constitutional Law (Oregon State Bar Legal Publications, 2nd ed. 2022).

will look at sources available to voters at the time the petition was adopted. Table 4.5 gives you some sources to use to find voter intent.

Table 4.5. Examples of Voter Intent

Source	Location
Ballot title	Initiative, Referendum, and Referral Search, Election Division, Oregon Secretary of State[9]
Voter pamphlet statements	• Election History, Oregon Secretary of State website[10] • Oregon Supreme Court or Multnomah County Law Libraries (older pamphlets)
Newspaper articles and editorials	Historic Oregon Newspapers database[11]

The most useful resource is the voter pamphlet. A voter pamphlet contains

- Text of the measure
- Ballot title: summary of the measure
- Statements for and against the measure

Older voter pamphlets are available at the Oregon Supreme Court and the Multnomah County law libraries.

Referrals are amendments to the constitution that the legislature passed and then submitted to the voters for approval. To determine the historical circumstances, you should look at both the voters' intent when they approved the referral and the legislators' intent when they passed the legislation. Determining the voters' intent for a referendum requires consulting the same sources as one would for the initiatives (see above). To find legislative history materials that show legislative intent, please see Chapter 6, Researching Oregon Legislative History.

9. https://egov.sos.state.or.us/elec/web_irr_search.search_form.
10. https://sos.oregon.gov/elections/Pages/electionhistory.aspx.
11. https://oregonnews.uoregon.edu/.

3. Exceptions

Some constitutional provisions do not follow the Priest Framework. Provisions that are identical to U.S. Constitution provisions may follow the federal court interpretations. Also, sections 8, 9 and 20 of Article I have been interpreted on a case-by-case basis.

Constitutional interpretation is complicated. In addition to reading the cases, you might also want to consult a secondary source. Some useful books and articles on the Oregon Constitution include:

- *Oregon Constitutional Law* (OSB Legal Pubs 2022),
- Jack L. Landau, *An Introduction to Oregon Constitutional Interpretation*, 55 Willamette L Rev 261 (2019), and
- *Interpreting Oregon Law*, chapter 7 (OSB Legal Pubs 2009).

IV. The Initiative, Referral, and Referendum

Under the Oregon Constitution, voters can directly change the *Oregon Revised Statutes* and the Oregon Constitution by initiative, referendum or referral.

- **Initiative:** voter proposed petition that is submitted to the voters for approval.
- **Referral:** governing body adopts a resolution that is submitted to the voters for approval.
- **Referendum:** voter rejection of legislation adopted by the Legislative Assembly.

The constitution can be amended only by initiative or referral. For an initiative, petitioners collect signatures to get a prospective initiative on the ballot, then the citizens vote on the initiative during the general election. For a referral, both houses of the legislature must approve referring a change to the constitution to the voters, and then the voters decide during the general election.

A. Initiative Process

Table 4.6 shows the voter initiative process in Oregon.

Table 4.6. Voter Initiative Process

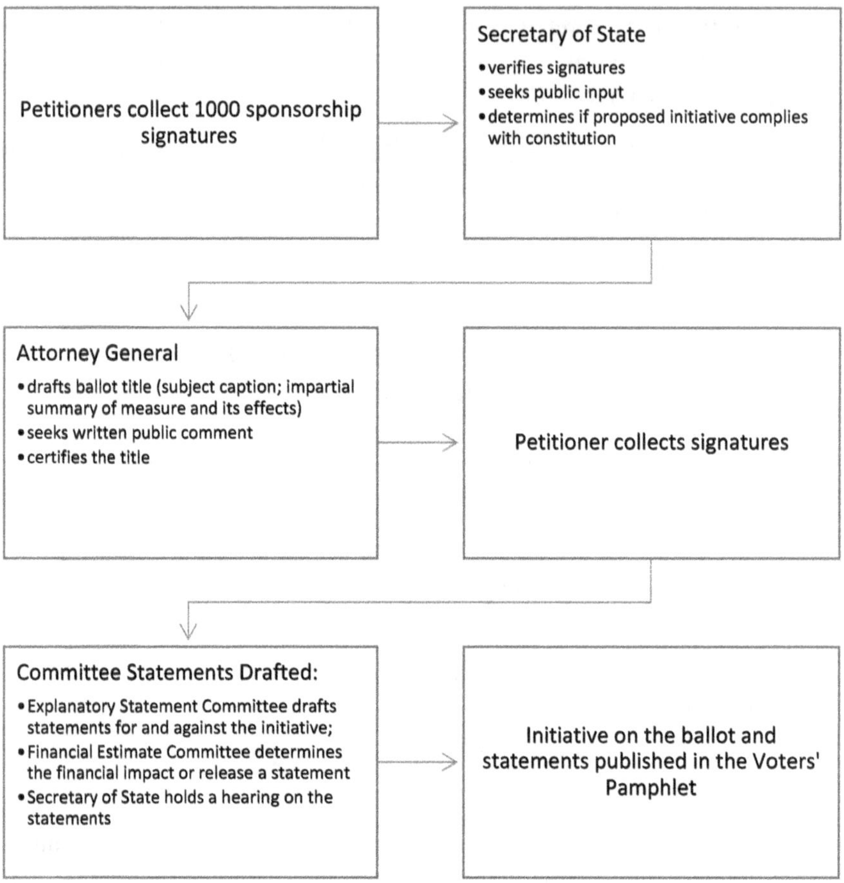

The Oregon Secretary of State's webpage provides detailed guidance on the process to get a measure on the ballot. In the Voting and Elections section of the website, select Initiatives, Referendums, Referrals and Recall and Make or

Change State Law from the left menu.[12] This page provides forms and manuals for petitioners.

The number of signatures that a petitioner must collect depends on the type of initiative and the number of votes for governor in the most recent election. For a constitutional initiative, a petitioner must collect eight percent of the number of votes most recently cast for governor, and for a statutory initiative, the petitioner must collect six percent.[13]

The referral process is slightly different. A referral does not require signature collection. The legislature can write the ballot title and summary or let the Attorney General draft and certify the ballot title. A final difference is that members of the legislature draft the statement in support of the measure that appears in the voters' pamphlet.

For a referendum, the petitioners must get approval from the Secretary of State and collect signatures within 90 days of the legislature's adjournment. They must collect four percent of the number of votes most recently cast for governor. Once the referendum is on the ballot, the act will not be effective until after the voters approve it in a general election.

B. Finding Measures

To find current and future measures, go to the Initiatives, Referendums, Referrals and Recall page in the Voting & Elections section of the Oregon Secretary of State's website.[14] See Table 4.7 for the location of these sources.

12. Initiatives, Referendums, Referrals and Recall: Make or Change the Law, OREGON SECRETARY OF STATE, https://sos.oregon.gov/elections/Pages/statelaw.aspx. See also Legislative Policy and Research Office, "Direct Democracy in Oregon: Background Brief" (November 19, 2020), https://digitalcollections.library.oregon.gov/nodes/view/151750.

13. Oregon Constitution Art IV, sec 1.

14. https://sos.oregon.gov/elections/Pages/initiatives-referendums-referrals.aspx.

Table 4.7. Locations of Past Measures

Source	Location
Ballot title	Initiative, Referendum, and Referral Search, Election Division, Oregon Secretary of State website[15]
Voter pamphlet statements	Election History, Oregon Secretary of State website[16]

15. https://egov.sos.state.or.us/elec/web_irr_search.search_form.
16. https://sos.oregon.gov/elections/Pages/electionhistory.aspx.

Chapter 5

Finding and Using Statutes

CHAPTER GOALS

After reading this chapter, you will be able to

1. Effectively read statutes;
2. Find statutes in print and online;
3. Use statutes to find cases; and
4. Determine if a statutory section is still good law.

Statutes contain the laws created by legislators and affect many legal issues. A statute might define a client's rights or responsibilities, as in landlord-tenant law. Statutes may set mandates and penalties for noncompliance, such as payment of taxes. Other statutes may codify or alter the common law, address policy concerns, or dictate procedures in legal actions.

This chapter focuses on Oregon statutes including, how to find statutes and how to find cases interpreting statutes on Lexis, Westlaw, and the Oregon Legislature's website.

I. Enacted Law in Oregon

Laws enacted by the legislature are first published individually as slip laws, then chronologically as session laws, and finally organized by subject in statutory codes. In Oregon, the session laws are published in a series titled *Oregon Laws* and the statutory code is published in a series titled *Oregon Revised Statutes*. Table 5.1 shows the publication process.

Table 5.1. Pattern of Publication

Bill		Session Law		Code
HB 2710 (2013)	→	*Oregon Laws* Or Laws 2013, ch 686, § 15	→	*Oregon Revised Statutes* ORS 837.380

A. Bills

There are two chambers in the Oregon Legislative Assembly, the House and the Senate. When a bill is introduced, it is assigned a number (the bill number). The bill has a title, such as "AN ACT Relating to drones" and will be divided into sections. It is identified by its chamber of origin, the bill number, and the session year. For example, a bill citation, HB 2710 (2013), refers to House Bill number 2710 that was introduced in the 2013 legislative session. Bills can be found online on the Oregon State Legislature's webpage.[1] Older bills back to 1955 are available in print at may Oregon law libraries.

B. *Oregon Laws* (Session Laws)

Oregon Laws publishes laws in chronological order. The volume number is the year of the legislative session. Once a bill passes the legislature and is signed by the governor, the secretary of state assigns a chapter number. For example, when HB 2710 (2013) passed, it was published in the *Oregon Laws*, and its citation is Or Laws 2013, ch 686, § 15. Or Laws is the abbreviation for *Oregon Laws*, and 2013 is the volume (session year). It was the 686th law passed during that session (chapter 686), and the specific portion of the law being cited is section 15.

The Oregon Legislature's website provides access to the *Oregon Laws* back to the mid-1990s.[2] Researchers can use the search box in the center of the page or browse by session year then chapter number. Supplemental documents, including indexes and tables are located in the right pane. A subscription database, HeinOnline, has scanned versions of the complete set of *Oregon Laws* in Hein's Session Laws Library. *Oregon Laws* are also published in print.

---

1. Bills and Laws Previous Session Bills, https://www.oregonlegislature.gov/bills_laws/Pages/previous-session-bills.aspx.
2. Oregon Laws, https://www.oregonlegislature.gov/bills_laws/Pages/Oregon-Laws.aspx.

While the *Oregon Laws* are the official text of the legislation, they are impractical to use. Because the laws are published in chronological order, it is difficult to determine if the law has been amended or repealed and to find laws governing the same topic. For this reason, researchers rely on statutory codes which organize the laws by topic.

For example, the language from Or Laws 2013, c. 686, § 15 can be found in the *Oregon Revised Statutes*, under

Title 62 Aviation

Chapter 837 Aircraft Operation

Section 380 Low flying unmanned aircraft systems; action for damages.

C. *Oregon Revised Statutes* (Code)

The current codification of Oregon statutes is called the *Oregon Revised Statutes* (ORS). The ORS is divided into sixty-two titles, each on a specific subject. The titles are subdivided into chapters, which are further subdivided into sections. Sections may be further divided into smaller units: subsections, paragraphs, subparagraphs, clauses, subclauses, and items. The chapter is the basic unit of classification in the ORS, and the sections within each chapter follow a typical design or pattern. Each chapter has a table of contents that you should use to identify important or relevant sections. Table 5.2 shows this basic design.

Table 5.2. Chapter Design

Definitions section(s)	definitions of terms that apply throughout the chapter
Principle section(s)	general rules and possibly exceptions or exemptions
Enforcement section(s)	how the rules will be implemented and enforced (delegation of authority to an agency, private litigation, etc.)
Technical section(s)	severability provision, effective date, savings provisions, sunset provisions
Penalty section(s)	Criminal and/or civil penalties for violating the rules of the chapter

The numbering system for the ORS is the chapter number, a decimal point, and the section number (ex. 837.380). The citation should be ORS followed by this number (i.e., ORS 837.380). Occasionally, the section number is followed by the subsection and paragraph in parenthesis: ORS 837.380 (1)(b).

The ORS is compiled and published by the Oregon Legislative Counsel. The official version is published in print. An unofficial version is available on the Oregon Legislature's website.[3] Both Lexis and Westlaw have unofficial versions of the ORS. West also has a print version, *West's Oregon Revised Statutes Annotated* (WORSA). Table 5.3 provides ORS locations.

Table 5.3. ORS Locations

Print	Online
ORS (Official)	Oregon State Legislature (free)[4]
WORSA	Westlaw
Lexis Oregon Statutes	Lexis

The ORS also contains some court rules. Court rules govern litigation practice from the filing of initial pleadings through the final appeal. The Evidence Code can be found in chapter 40 of the ORS, and the rules of criminal procedure are codified in chapter 136. The Oregon Rules of Civil Procedure (ORCP) are not codified in the ORS, but they are still enacted law.[5] Other court rules are written by the courts. For more on these types of court rules, see section VII of this Chapter.

---

3. *Oregon Revised Statutes*, https://www.oregonlegislature.gov/bills_laws/Pages/ORS.aspx.

4. *Id.*

5. The 1979 Legislature enacted the ORCP and can amend, repeal, or supplement the ORCP through legislation. It also delegated the power to amend the ORCP to the Oregon Council on Court Procedures. The Council submits proposed amendments to the legislature at the beginning of each session, and unless the legislature changes the proposed amendments during the session, they become law.

II. Overview of the statutory research process

Table 5.4. Steps in the Statutory Research Process

1. Find the statute	Use a citation Use a secondary source Browse a table of contents Consult an index Search
2. Read the statute	Read critically, with professional purpose Look at table of contents for surrounding sections
3. Find cases analyzing the statute	Use annotations Use citators
4. Update the statute	Check for new legislation Check for cases negatively affecting the statute

Table 5.4 provides the basic steps in the statutory research process. This part of this chapter will explain the steps for researching statutes: finding, reading, analyzing, and updating.

A. Finding Statutes

Table 5.5 lists the various methods for finding statutes.

Table 5.5. Methods for Finding Statutes

Use the statute citation
Find a citation in a secondary source
Browse the statutory code table of contents
Consult an index
Use a natural language or Boolean search

1. Use a Statute Citation

If you know the statute's citation, you can find the statute's text by locating the statutory code print volume, looking for the chapter number, and then looking within the chapter for the section number. For example, if the citation is ORS 837.380, look within chapter 837 for section 380. If you are looking online, you can type the citation into a search bar or use the citation to browse the appropriate chapter and section. Table 5.6 shows this process in specific online research providers.

Table 5.6. Steps for Finding Statutes by Citation (Example: ORS 837.380)

Print (ORS and WORSA)	• Go to the volume that contains 837 • Look within the volume for chapter 837 • Look within chapter 837 for section 380 (statute numbers are on the top outside corner of each page)
Oregon State Legislature's site	• Select the volume that has chapter 837 • Select the title number that has chapter 837 • Select chapter 837 • Scroll down to 837.380
Lexis or Westlaw	In the global search box, type *ors 837.380*

If the citation is unknown, you can use multiple methods to find a statute or several statutes on point: consult a secondary source on the legal topic,[6] browse the table of contents, look up legal terms in a statute index, or search the ORS. Use every method to ensure that you do not miss any relevant statutes.

2. Browse a Table of Contents

Because statutes are organized by subject, the table of contents can be an effective approach for finding a statute. First identify the broadest legal category for your issue from the list of volumes or titles, then narrow down to the most relevant chapter then the most relevant section(s) within that chapter. Table 5.7 details this process in the various ORS locations.

6. For more on locating secondary sources, see Chapter 3.

Table 5.7. Steps for Browsing a Statutory Table of Contents

ORS (official print), WORSA (print), Oregon State Legislature's website	• Identify the relevant volume, title, and chapter • At the beginning of each chapter, find the table of contents for the chapter's sections
Lexis	• From the main page, select the State tab then the Oregon link • Scroll down to Statutes & Legislation and select OR—LexisNexis® Oregon Annotated Statutes • Select the plus sign next to a relevant title, chapter and sections
Westlaw	• From the main page, select the State Materials tab, then the Oregon link • Scroll down to Statutes and Court Rules and select Oregon Statutes & Court Rules • Choose a relevant title and chapter • Select the relevant sections

3. Consult an Index

When it is unclear where a particular topic falls in the table of contents, an index can be very useful. An index is an alphabetical list of legal topics and subtopics and the corresponding location in the ORS. (See Table 5.8 for the location of these indexes.) An index will have a wide range of topics, and the alphabetical arrangement makes it easy to navigate.

Table 5.8. Location of ORS Indexes

ORS (print) WORSA (print)	Go to the index volumes at the end of the set
Oregon State Legislature's website (free)	Go to the ORS General Index box in the right pane
Westlaw	Go to the Oregon Statutes & Court Rules page. In the right panel under Tools & Resources, select Index—Oregon Statutes

Sometimes the index entry is very long and overwhelming. In these cases, look for a Generally or Definitions subtopic. Once you find an ORS section on point, remember to consult the table of contents at the beginning of the section's chapter to find other relevant sections. You can also use the ORS Popular Name Table. This table allows researchers to look up the common name of the legislation and determine where it was codified.

4. Search the ORS

The final method of finding a statute is to search the ORS. On Lexis and Westlaw, use the search box at the top of the screen on the ORS table of contents. To limit the search to specific portions of the ORS check the boxes next to the title or chapter in the table of contents. On the Oregon State Legislature's website, the ORS search will search the entire text of the ORS, but it is free. Table 5.9 shows the search features for these various databases.

Statutory language is exact: synonyms are rarely used, and words are not repeated. As a result, searching the text of the ORS can be frustrating. On Westlaw and Lexis, a statute search will automatically include the statute text and the text of the annotations, which sometimes yields better results. If you want to search only the statute text, you can select the "advanced" link next to the search box. The advanced search screen allows you to search by field, including "Statutory Text" on Westlaw and "unannotated" on Lexis. On the Oregon State Legislature's page, you can search either the statutory text or the annotation text, not both.

Table 5.9. Databases with Search Features

Oregon Legislature's Website (free)	Use the search box in the middle of the screen, above the Table of Contents
Lexis	• Use the search box at the top of the screen • Limit the search to portions of the ORS by checking boxes in the table of contents • Select Advanced Search next to the search box for more search features
Westlaw	• Use the search box at the top of the screen • Limit the search to portions of the ORS by checking boxes in the table of contents • Select Advanced next to the search box for more search features

B. Reading, Applying, and Interpreting Statutes

Using statutes in legal work requires careful reading of the text, referring to related statutes, and analyzing the cases that involve those statutes. Disputes may arise over how to apply the statute to the facts of a current situation or how to interpret the meaning of the statute itself.

1. Reading Statutes

Statutory language can be very complex and takes time and effort to understand. Consider breaking down passages into elements by listing key ideas/requirements. Connecting words and punctuation will guide you in understanding relationships between different requirements of the section. Table 5.10 give you the meanings of common connecting words in statutes.

Table 5.10. Statutory Language

Statutory Term	Meaning
And	All requirements must be present
Or	Only one requirement is needed
Shall	Requires action
May	Permissive

In reading the text of a statute, you must also follow the rules of construction mandated by statute or case law:

- Courts must read statutes exactly as written without adding or deleting anything. ORS 174.010.
- If a general provision and particular provision are inconsistent, the particular provision controls. ORS 174.020(b).
- Words of common usage are to be given their "plain, natural, and ordinary meaning." *PGE v. Bureau of Labor & Industry*, 317 Or. 606, 611 (1993).
- Understanding the context of a statutory provision includes reading other sections of the same statute and other related statutes. *Id.*; *Southern Pacific Trans. Co. v. Dept. of Rev.*, 316 Or. 495, 498 (1993); *Sanders v. Oregon Pacific States Ins. Co.*, 314 Or. 521, 527 (1992).

2. Applying and Interpreting Statutes

Most often in legal work, applying a statute will mean reading its words carefully, referring to related statutes, analyzing cases that involve the statute, and applying it to the facts of your client's situation. In these circumstances, the issue is how the statute applies to the current situation, not the meaning of the statute. To read more about finding cases applying and analyzing a statute, see section IV of this chapter.

Sometimes, however, parties disagree over the meaning of the statute, so the dispute concerns how the statutory language is interpreted. In these cases, Oregon Supreme Court decisions provide a three-part template for statutory interpretation:

a. Examine the text and context of the statute,

b. Review the legislative history of the statute, and

c. Consider general maxims of statutory construction.

The first level of analysis involves reading the text of the statute and understanding its context, as discussed in the previous subsection. If the text of the statute has only one meaning, the court may conclude the inquiry. In the second level of analysis the court reviews the legislative history of the statute. Legislative history research is covered in Chapter 6. If the meaning is still ambiguous, a court follows the "general maxims of statutory construction," also known as canons of construction. (See Table 5.11 for these maxims.) Canons of construction are most often judicially created and based on assumptions about what judges think the legislature would prefer.[7]

7. Jack L. Landau, *Oregon Statutory Construction*, 97 Or. L. Rev. 583, 711 (2018).

Table 5.11. Maxims of Statutory Construction

Unreasonable Results Canon	When a statute can reasonably be interpreted in two ways, but one would lead to absurd results, the court will choose the other interpretation.[8]
Avoidance Canon	When competing reasonable interpretations arise, but one raises constitutional issues, the court will favor the construction that avoids constitutional issues.[9]
Natural Rights Canon	"Where a statute is equally susceptible of two interpretations, one in favor of a natural right and the other against it, the former is to prevail."[10]

Statutory construction can be very difficult, and this discussion has provided only a brief overview. An extensive explanation of Oregon's process is *Oregon Statutory Construction*, by retired Oregon Supreme Court Justice Jack Landau.[11]

C. Finding Cases That Apply the Statute

After locating (and reading!) a relevant statute, you should look for cases that help you analyze the statute. The two primary tools for finding cases that refer to a statute are annotations and citators.

1. Look for Annotations

Annotations are brief summaries of decisions by Oregon courts that reference a particular statute. They are written by the publisher's staff, so they are not official summaries. They will include the full citation to the case which you can then look up. When a statute has a lot of annotations, they may be organized topically. Table 5.12 gives you where to find annotations.

8. *Id.* at 711–12.
9. *Id.* at 717.
10. ORS 174.030.
11. *See supra* note 7.

Table 5.12. Where to Find Annotations

ORS (print)	Separate volume at the end of the set
WORSA (print)	After the statute section, under Notes of Decisions
Oregon State Legislature's website (free)	Go to the Bills and Laws tab. In the left pane, under *Oregon Revised Statutes*, select ORS Annotations.
Westlaw	At the top of the relevant statute's page, select the Notes of Decisions tab.
Lexis	On the relevant statute's page, scroll down to Notes to Decisions.

2. Use a Citator

Citators provide lists of cases that cite a statute. You can use filters to narrow the citator list by jurisdiction, date, and reported status (i.e., whether the case is published/reported or unpublished/unreported). One of the most useful features of citators is the ability to search the full text of the citing cases. So, you can search for cases that cited your statute that had similar facts. For example, if you are researching the DUII statute (ORS 813.010), you can use the citator to find a list of cases that cited the statute. You can then search across those cases to narrow the list to cases involving a specific drug.

The two major citators are Shepard's on Lexis and KeyCite on Westlaw (see Table 5.13).

Table 5.13. Locating Citators

Lexis	At the top of the relevant statute's page, select Citing Decisions. The filters are in the left pane
Westlaw	At the top of the relevant statute's page, hover over the Citing References tab and select Cases from the dropdown menu. To view the filters, select Filters in the left pane

D. Updating Statutes

Statutes or sections of statutes can change. Legislatures may amend them by refining or changing the language of the section. If the legislature repeals a statute, it ceases to be in force and is removed from the code. Courts may also determine that a statute or portion of a statute is unconstitutional. To determine if a statute is still good law, a researcher needs to update or validate it.

1. What Is the Publication Date?

Table 5.14. Determining If Statute Is Current

ORS and Oregon Legislature's Website	The year will be on the binding or in the title (i.e., ORS 2023 Edition).
WORSA	Check the year on the title page of the volume. Check the year on the title page of the supplement in the back of the volume (also called the pocket part).
Lexis	Within a statute section, look directly underneath the statute number in the center of the page.
Westlaw	Within a statute section, select Currency under the title of the statute or scroll to the bottom of the page.

First, you need to determine when your ORS statute was published, or how current it is. The official print version and the Oregon State Legislature's online version of the ORS are published every two years. Lexis and Westlaw are regularly updated. WORSA, West's print version of the ORS, is updated with an insert in the back of the volume which is called a pocket part. Table 5.14 shows how to determine if a statute is current.

2. Are There New or Pending Amendments?

Table 5.15. Finding New or Pending Amendments

Oregon State Legislature's Website	• On the ORS page, read the center box. It will explain how to best update the ORS. • Go to the Statutes Affected by Measure box in the right pane. • Locate the referenced bill or Oregon Laws citation using the links in the left pane.
Lexis	• In the right pane of statute, under the Compare Versions box, look for a yellow or red upside-down triangle with an exclamation point in the right pane. • Select the link next to the triangle to view the changes or the pending legislation.
Westlaw	• On the statute's page, there will be a yellow or red flag to the left of the statute citation at the top of the page. • Hover over the History tab at the top of the page, then select Validity from the dropdown menu.

Once you determine the statute's publication date, you can check to see if there have been any amendments to the statute since it was published. Table 5.15 provides an overview of this process. When you are using the Oregon State Legislature's website, the language in the center box will explain how best to determine if your statute has been amended since the publication date. Typically, you will consult the Statutes Affected by Measures table which is located on the left frame under ORS Documents. You can look up the number of the statute, and the table will indicate whether it was amended or repealed by recent legislation and provide that legislation's session law citation (*Oregon Laws* chapter and section) and the bill number. Then, you can locate the bill or session law using the left pane of the website.

Lexis and Westlaw update their versions of the ORS immediately; however, if the new amendments do not go into effect immediately, Lexis and Westlaw will notify users of the imminent change. Lexis will have a yellow or red upside-down triangle with an exclamation point in the right pane, under the "Compare Versions" box. If you select the Compare Versions box, you can see how the amendments change the current language (the deleted language is crossed out and the new language is highlighted). Westlaw will have a yellow or red flag to the left of the statute. Click on the flag to find an explanation of the amendment or proposed amendment and a link to the bill or session law affecting the statute.

3. Did a Case Find the Statute Unconstitutional?

Another way a statute may cease to be good law is if a court determines that it violates the constitution. To find those cases, use the citators on Lexis (Shepard's) and Westlaw (KeyCite). If a case treats a statute negatively, you will see a red or yellow icon next to the citation in the top left corner. Table 5.16 details this process.

Table 5.16. Finding Negative Treatment of a Statute

Lexis (Shepard's)	1. If there are negative cases, an inverted red or yellow triangle with exclamation point will appear next to the ORS citation at the top of the page. 2. Go to the right pane, under Shepard's and Citing Decisions, select either Warning or Caution to view a list of the negative cases.
Westlaw (KeyCite)	1. If there are negative cases, a red or yellow flag will appear next to the ORS citation at the top of the page. 2. Select the flag, and it will take you to the Validity section of the History tab. The negative cases will be listed.

III. Court Rules

Court rules govern litigation practice from the filing of initial pleadings through the final appeal. Rules dictate litigation details ranging from the correct caption for pleadings to the standard for summary judgment. Court rules like the Oregon Rules of Civil Procedure and the Uniform Trial Court Rules are primary authority even when the court or legislature responsible for them has delegated rulemaking power to a council, committee, or other body. Success in litigation may depend as much on compliance with these rules as with the merit of the claim.

Table 5.17. Locating Court Rules Online

Oregon Courts Rules Center website[12]
Oregon State Legislature's website[13]
Lexis: On the Oregon page, select OR—Oregon Local, State & Federal Court Rules
Westlaw: On the Oregon page, select Oregon Statutes & Court Rules or Oregon Rules of Civil Procedure

The website of the Oregon courts links to court rules.[14] The resulting page includes links to most of the rules listed above as well to any Supplementary Local Rules (SLR) adopted by an Oregon trial court. These rules might also appear on the individual court's website. To illustrate, the Third Judicial Circuit (Marion County, where Salem is located) sets out in its SLR the hours the court is open, the requirements for being approved by the court as a mediator, and many other details. Use the index or table of contents provided with each set of rules to locate particular rules that affect your work.

12. https://www.courts.oregon.gov/rules/Pages/default.aspx.

13. https://www.oregonlegislature.gov/bills_laws. The Oregon Rules of Civil Procedure (ORCP) are located in the left panel under *Oregon Revised Statutes*. The Evidence Code and Rules of Criminal Procedure are in the ORS volumes 1 and 4, respectively.

14. From courts.oregon.gov, click on "Forms/Rules/Fees" at the top of the page, and then select "Rules Center."

In addition to the Oregon courts website, rules are available through several other sources, four of which are described below. Be sure that you are working with the current rule, whether working with print or online sources.

First, court rules are frequently published in statutory codifications, both in print and in online resources.

Second, a deskbook is a print compilation of rules. The following rules are among those published in *Oregon Rules of Court: State*, published annually by West:

Oregon Rules of Civil Procedure
Evidence Code[15]
Oregon Rules of Appellate Procedure
Uniform Trial Court Rules
Rules of the Oregon Tax Court

Third, Lexis provides an online database that contains Oregon local, state, and federal rules. Westlaw includes many court rules in databases with state statutes.

Fourth, Westlaw has separate databases solely containing Oregon Rules of Civil Procedure and the Evidence Code. You can find those from the homepage, by typing the name of the code into the universal search bar and scrolling through the suggested results to "Content Pages" for the desired set of rules. Table 5.17 shows the location of court rules.

Rules are written in outline form like statutes, and they should be read like statutes. Read each word carefully, refer to cross-referenced rules, and scan other rules nearby to see whether they are related. After locating a rule on point, find cases that apply the rule by searching annotations published with the rule or by searching a topical index. Never assume that an Oregon rule mirrors its federal counterpart or that cases applying a federal rule will be relevant to application of an Oregon rule.

The text of some rules is accompanied by commentary by the committee charged with drafting or modifying the rules. The commentary is persuasive authority.

15. Rules 100 to 1008 are codified in Chapter 40 of the *Oregon Revised Statutes*.

Chapter 6

Researching Oregon Legislative History

CHAPTER GOALS:

After reading this chapter, you will be able to

1. Explain the Oregon legislative process;
2. Identify legislative documents;
3. Compile legislative histories; and
4. Describe how to track new legislation.

While litigation generally involves laws that are in force, sometimes lawyers will need to consult documents created during the process in which a bill becomes a law. For example, when a statute's language is ambiguous, a court might initially look at whether other statutes, cases, or administrative agency regulations have addressed the ambiguity. If those sources do not help, the court may look at documents indicating what the legislators intended the language to mean when they wrote, discussed, and passed the bill.[1] Other times, a lawyer might track current legislation that will, if passed, affect a client's interests.

Legislative history research involves compiling the documents or other materials generated as a bill becomes a law. This chapter will begin with an overview of the legislative process in Oregon and the different documents involved with that process. Next, the chapter will explain how to compile those documents for a statute that has already been enacted (i.e., compiling a legislative history). Finally, the chapter will describe the process of bill tracking or monitoring the status of a current bill that may or may not ultimately be enacted.

1. ORS § 174.020.

I. The Legislative Process

The Oregon Legislative Assembly is comprised of two chambers: the Senate and the House of Representatives. The Senate has thirty members, and the House has sixty members. The Assembly meets annually, although sessions during odd-numbered years are longer.

The general process of enacting and amending laws in Oregon begins with the introduction of a bill in one of the chambers. The bill is given a bill number. Regular bills introduced in the Oregon House of Representatives begin with HB ("House Bill") while bills introduced in the Senate begin with SB ("Senate Bill"). The bill is assigned to a committee which will hold public hearings and work sessions. The committee might make amendments to the bill, and then it will vote on whether the bill should move forward to the main body. If the vote is successful, the bill goes to the floor of the chamber where it is debated and then voted on. Bills can be amended only in committees, so it may be sent back to committee for amendments. Otherwise, it will be voted on. If the bill passes, it moves to the next chamber which follows the same process. If the second chamber passes the bill without amendments, it goes to the governor to sign. If it has been amended by the second chamber, then it returns to the first chamber. If that chamber agrees with the amendments, then it proceeds to the governor. If it does not agree, then the bill is sent to a conference committee to reconcile the differences. The version of the conference bill must pass both chambers, then it goes to the governor to sign. Table 6.1 shows the process of a bill becoming a law.

II. Legislative Documents

Each step of the legislative process produces materials and documents. This section focuses on the different materials and where they are located. The next section, Compiling Legislative History, will focus on how to find legislative materials connected to a statute.

Legislative materials and documents are located in a variety of places. Online, you will typically consult a number of pages on the Oregon State Legislature's website. The database for more recent Oregon legislative information is OLIS ("Oregon Legislative Information System").[2] Older legislative information may be available on the State Archives website. The database for the State

2. https://olis.oregonlegislature.gov.

Table 6.1. How a Bill Becomes a Law

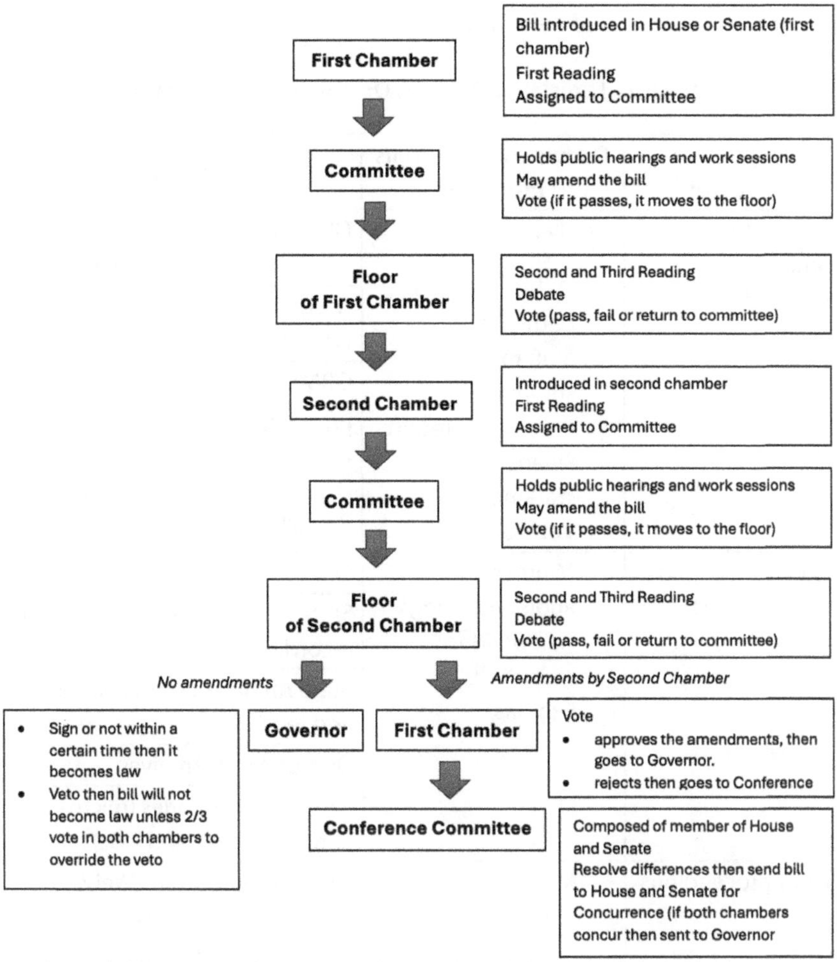

Archives is also referred to as State Archives Online Holdings or the ORMS.[3] Often materials are not available online, which requires a visit to an Oregon law library and the State Archives building in Salem.[4]

3. https://records.sos.state.or.us.

4. The Oregon State Archives is located at 800 Summer Street N.E., Salem, Oregon. The telephone number for the reference room is (503) 373-0701, extension 1, and the email address is reference.archives@state.or.us.

Because each of these places hold different materials, you should first identify the documents you need and where to find them. Table 6.2 shows the location for documents produced in each step in the legislative process:

Table 6.2. Legislative Process, Documents, and Location

<table>
<tr><th>Legislative Activity</th><th>Documents/Materials Produced</th><th>Location</th></tr>
<tr><td rowspan="4">Bill is introduced, amended, enacted</td><td rowspan="4">Bill File:
• Different versions of the bill
• Staff measure summary
• Committee report
• Financial impact statements
• Vote tallies</td><td>OLIS: on the bill's page, select the Text tab and the Analysis tab</td></tr>
<tr><td>Oregon State Legislature's website[5]</td></tr>
<tr><td>ORMS</td></tr>
<tr><td>Print (older bills):
• State Archives
• Oregon law libraries (older bills)</td></tr>
<tr><td rowspan="5">Committee holds hearings and votes</td><td rowspan="5">• Minutes and audio/video logs
• Audio/video recordings
• Exhibits</td><td>OLIS</td></tr>
<tr><td>State Archives Website (logs and recordings)</td></tr>
<tr><td>State Archives ORMS (exhibits and logs)[6]</td></tr>
<tr><td>Oregon State Archives</td></tr>
<tr><td>Oregon law libraries (microfilmed minutes and logs)</td></tr>
<tr><td>Floor proceedings</td><td>• Minutes
• Recordings</td><td>Oregon Legislature's Website
• Journals of the House and Senate (minutes)
• Citizen Engagement tab (recordings)[7]</td></tr>
</table>

5. https://www.oregonlegislature.gov/bills_laws/Pages/previous-session-bills.aspx.

6. https://sos.oregon.gov/archives/Pages/records/legislative_minutes.aspx.

7. https://www.oregonlegislature.gov/citizen_engagement/Pages/Legislative-Video.aspx.

<table>
<tr><td rowspan="3">Governor signs or vetoes</td><td rowspan="3">• Signing letter
• Vetoing statement</td><td>Current governor's website[8]</td></tr>
<tr><td>State Archives Governor's Records Guides[9]</td></tr>
<tr><td>House and Senate Journals (veto statements)</td></tr>
</table>

A. Original Bill File

The bill file contains the original text of the bill, amended versions of the bill (engrossed bills) and, if the bill passes, the final version of the bill (enrolled bill). The bill file may also contain other documents, including:

1. A staff measure summary (previously called a staff analysis) which explains the bill in clear, concise language.
2. A committee report which is a form that records the committee's actions on the bill.
3. Financial analysis statements, such as a fiscal impact statement or a revenue impact statement.
4. Tallies of the votes on the floor of each chamber.

The original bill files are kept at the Oregon State Archives. Bill files for older measures may be in print form at law libraries. After 2007, many of the documents in the bill file are available online on OLIS. On the main page for the bill, the "Text" tab has the different versions of the bill, and the "Analysis" tab links to the staff measure summaries, revenue impact statements, fiscal impact statements and any budget reports. On the Oregon Legislature's website, you can find the original, amended and final versions of bills since 1995.[10]

B. Committee Work

Much of Oregon's legislative work takes place in committees. Committees will hold public hearings and work sessions on the bill. Since 1957, these hearings and work sessions have been recorded, but there are no transcripts of the recordings. Instead, researchers can consult minutes or logs to determine who spoke when, then listen or view the recordings. Committees may also refer to various exhibits that a researcher should consult.

---

8. https://www.oregon.gov/gov/pages/resources.aspx.
9. https://sos.oregon.gov/archives/Pages/records/governors_guides.aspx.
10. *See supra* note 3.

1. Committee Minutes and Audio and Video Logs

Committee minutes and audio/video logs provide basic information about the hearing or work session activity. They are not transcripts. Committee minutes are summaries noting each person who spoke and the substance of the person's remarks. Audio logs began in 2007, and video recording logs began in 2014. The logs are simply lists of the speakers without summaries.

Minutes and logs from 1991 forward are available at the Oregon State Archives website. Minutes from 1926 through the mid-1990s are available in microfilm format at some university law libraries and some county law libraries.

2. Committee Audio and Video Recordings

Audio recordings of committee hearings and work sessions have been available since 1957. While the state currently uses digital audio recordings, many types of media have been used such as reel-to-reel tapes, dictation tapes, and cassettes.

Use the committee minutes or log to find the date and time the bill was discussed. The minutes and logs also can be helpful as you listen to the recording because they identify the different speakers.

Recent digital audio recordings are available from OLIS. From the bills main page, scroll down and select Measure History. From the list of dates and activities, public hearings and work sessions will be hyperlinked. Following the links will lead to a committee page that may have an agenda, meeting materials, or a log. To access the recording, look up the date on the right side of the screen and select the play icon next to the date.

3. Exhibits

Legislators, committee staff, or those testifying at public hearings may submit exhibits. These might include proposed amendments to a bill, written testimony submitted during consideration of the bill, reports related to the bill and even letters from interested parties. Sometimes, there are reports prepared by interim committees that met between regular sessions of the legislature.

Oregon State Archives will have the most comprehensive collection of exhibits. They are generally stored in three-ring binders. More recent exhibits may be found on OLIS. On the main page for your bill, select the "Meeting Materials/Exhibits" tab. Older exhibits, up to the mid-1990s, are located in microfilm in some law libraries.

C. Floor Proceedings

Once a bill is passed by the committee, it goes to the full chamber (House or Senate) for a second and third reading. The legislators may debate the bill and vote to pass or not pass. Since amendments can only take place at the committee stage, they may also vote to send the bill back to committee. Researchers may be interested in audio recordings of the chamber debates and the journals of the House and Senate.

1. Recordings of the Chamber Debates

Audio recordings of the debate on the floor of each chamber are available, beginning in 1963 for the House and in 1973 for the Senate. For sessions from 1999 to present, researchers can access recordings of chamber debates by going to the Oregon Legislature's website, hovering over the "Get Involved" tab and selecting "Legislative Meetings."[11] Audio tabs for prior sessions are kept at the Oregon State Archives.

2. Journals of the House and Senate

The journals of the House and Senate record the actions of each chamber when it is in session. Included in these journals are votes on bills and other measures, explanations of votes by representatives, and messages from the Governor.

Recent versions of the journals can be found on the Oregon Legislature's website. For the Senate Journals, hover over the "Senate" tab and select "Secretary of the Senate."[12] Scroll down to the Senate Journals box on the right side of the page. For the House Journals, hover over the "House" tab, and select "Chief Clerk of the House." In the left pane, select "Journals & Floor Proceedings."[13]

D. Governor's Actions

Once a bill passes both chambers, it is enrolled and sent to the Governor. If the Governor signs the bill or does not sign the bill within a certain period, it becomes law. If the Governor vetoes the bill, it will not become law unless a

---

11. https://www.oregonlegislature.gov/citizen_engagement/Pages/Legislative-Video.aspx.

12. https://www.oregonlegislature.gov/secretary-of-senate/.

13. https://www.oregonlegislature.gov/chief-clerk/Pages/journals-daily-proceedings.aspx.

two-thirds vote in both chambers overrides the veto. Sometimes the Governor will issue a signing or veto statement.

Statements can be found on the current governor's website, under the "Resources" tab.[14] Statements from previous governors are on the State Archives Governor's Records Guides webpage.[15] Some veto statements are published in the journals of the House and Senate, discussed above.

III. Compiling Legislative Histories

Compiling a legislative history is gathering all the legislative materials for a bill that was enacted. Lawyers will do this when the meaning of a statute is not clear or when the meaning is at issue in litigation. Reviewing the legislative history assists in the effort to determine the legislature's intent in enacting the statute.[16]

In Oregon legislative history research, you are primarily looking for the following:

1. Committee minutes or audio/video logs for the meetings of the committees that considered the bill;
2. Recordings of the committee meetings;
3. Any exhibits;
4. The original bill file;
5. Recordings of the floor proceedings for each chamber; and
6. Statements in the journals of the House and Senate.

Oregon courts often cite the recordings of committee meetings and information from the bill file, so those materials are particularly important.

---

14. Governor of Oregon : Resources: State of Oregon, https://www.oregon.gov/gov/pages/resources.aspx.

15. Governor's Records Guides, *supra* note 4.

16. *See* ORS 174.020 (instructing courts to "pursue the intention of the legislature if possible" in construing statutes); *see also PGE v. Bureau of Lab. And Indus.*, 317 Or 606, 611–12 (1993); Hon. Jack L. Landau, *Oregon Statutory Construction*, 97 Or L Rev 583 (2019).

Table 6.3. Process for Compiling a Legislative History

1. Find the statute section in question and go to the source note at the end of the statute text.
2. Look up the *Oregon Laws* citations listed in the source note to determine when the language was first added; note the bill number at the beginning of the *Oregon Laws* chapter.
3. See if the State Archives compiled a legislative tracing.
4. Use the bill number to find the measure history; note the committees and dates of meetings and the dates of floor activity.
5. Look up the Committee activity (minutes/logs, recordings and exhibits).

To compile a legislative history, use the statute to find the session law (*Oregon Laws*) which then leads to the bill number. The bill number is used to find the legislative documents. If the bill was recent, most of the materials can be found online; however, older legislation often requires a trip to the State Archives building in Salem.[17] Table 6.3 outlines the process for compiling a legislative history.

A. Step One: Find the Statute's Source Note

The process of compiling a legislative history begins with the statute section in question. At the end of the text, locate a source note which provides the citations to the various Oregon Laws that created or amended the language of that section. The note is always after the text; however, different publishers might give it a heading like "History" or "Credits," or it will be in brackets.

17. The Oregon State Archives is located at 800 Summer Street N.E., Salem, Oregon. The telephone number for the reference room is (503) 373-0701, extension 1, and the email address is reference.archives@state.or.us.

The following example shows the source note for ORS 837.380:

[2013 c. 686 § 15; 2015 c. 315 § 11; 2016 c. 72 § 10]

2016 c. 72 § 10 is a citation to *Oregon Laws. Oregon Laws* publishes the enacted bills for each legislative session in chronological order based on the date of enactment. The first citation in the source note refers to the original act, and each subsequent amendment is separated by semicolons. The first citation in the source note example is 2013 c. 686 § 15 which means that ORS 837.380 was enacted in 2013 by Oregon Law chapter 686, section 15. The second citation, 2015 c. 315 § 11 indicates that ORS § 837.380 was amended in 2015 by Oregon Law 315, section 11.

The source notes in the ORS provide information only back to 1953. If nothing appears in a history note, refer to Prior Legislative History which was published with the 1953 edition of the ORS. In these situations, it is likely that no legislative history documentation exists.

B. Step Two: Use the Source Note to Find the Bill Number

Next, look up each *Oregon Laws* citation listed in the source note to find when the language at issue was first added to the statute section. Both Lexis and Westlaw provide hypertext links in the source note to the *Oregon Laws*. You can then use the "find in page" feature to look up the language. The ORS on the Oregon Legislature's website does not provide links in the source note, so you must look up the *Oregon Laws*. The *Oregon Laws* are available on the Oregon Legislature's website, in HeinOnline's Session Law Library, and in print at Oregon law libraries.

When you find the language in question, go to the beginning of the chapter in *Oregon Laws* and note the bill number. For example, if you were looking at Oregon Laws 2016 chapter 72, section 10, you could find the bill number by going to the beginning of chapter 72. The following is an excerpt of *Oregon Laws* 2016, and HB 4066 is the bill number for the legislation (see Figure 6.1).

Figure 6.1. Excerpt of Oregon Laws 2016

CHAPTER 72

AN ACT HB 4066

Relating to unmanned aircraft systems; creating new provisions; amending ORS 163.700, 164.885, 498.128, 837.300, 837.360, 837.365 and 837.380; and declaring an emergency.

Be It Enacted by the People of the State of Oregon:

DEFINITION OF "UNMANNED AIRCRAFT SYSTEM"

SECTION 1. ORS 837.300 is amended to read:

837.300. As used in ORS 837.300 to 837.390 and 837.995:

[*(1) "Unmanned aircraft system" means an unmanned flying machine, commonly known as a drone. "Unmanned aircraft system" does not include a model aircraft as defined in section 336 of the FAA Modernization and Reform Act of 2012 (P.L. 112-95) as in effect on July 29, 2013.*]

C. Step Three: Look for a Legislative Tracing

Sometimes, the State Archives has already compiled the legislative materials for a bill. Whenever someone contacts the State Archives to request legislative materials, the reference staff compiles a tracing, meaning the staff determines which committees considered the bill and locates the minutes/logs from when the bill was discussed, including dates and page numbers. The staff also lists or summarizes related exhibits and compiles a list of committee audio recordings. This information is saved and made available to future researchers. Sometimes the online holdings include exhibits and audio recordings.

The State Archives online holdings are on a database called Oregon Records Management Solution (ORMS).[18] To find a legislative tracing, use the drop-down menu to select "Title" then in the box type the year and bill number, then search. Select the title of the relevant result and select "View/Download"

18. Oregon Records Management Solution (ORMS), https://records.sos.state.or.us/.

in the upper right corner to view the document. For more information on searching for legislative tracings, including how to order a legislative tracing, see the State Archives' Legislative Tracing webpage.[19]

D. Step Four: Find the Bill's Measure History

If there is not a legislative tracing, use the bill number to find the legislative documents. Begin by looking up the bill's measure history. For recent bills, go to OLIS.[20] Using the icons at the top right of the page, first select the "Session" icon and select the session year of your bill. Next, select the "Bills" icon and either type in your bill number or use the arrows to scroll down to your bill. Once on the bill's main page, scroll down and select "Measure History." The Measure History lists the dates and actions taken on the bill, from when it was introduced to when it was enacted. Note the committees that the bill was assigned to and the dates of the committees' public hearings and work sessions. Also note the dates of floor activity.

For example, if you wanted to find the measure history for 2016 *HB 4066*, go to OLIS, and using the "Session" icon at the top right of the page, select the 2016 regular session. Using the "Bills" icon, enter *HB 4066*. From the bill's Overview page, scroll down and select "Measure History." Figure 6.2 is a screenshot of the Measure History.

19. https://sos.oregon.gov/archives/Pages/records/legislative_tracings.aspx.
20. https://olis.oregonlegislature.gov/.

Figure 6.2. Measure History

Measure History	
1-27 (H)	Presession Released to the Public.
2-1 (H)	First reading. Referred to Speaker's desk.
2-1 (H)	Referred to Judiciary.
2-8 (H)	Public Hearing held.
2-10 (H)	Work Session held.
2-15 (H)	Recommendation: Do pass with amendments and be printed A-Engrossed.
2-16 (H)	Second reading.
2-17 (H)	Third reading. Carried by Huffman. Passed. Ayes, 59; Excused, 1--Barton.
2-18 (S)	First reading. Referred to President's desk.
2-18 (S)	Referred to Judiciary.
2-22 (S)	Public Hearing held.
2-23 (S)	Work Session held.
2-24 (S)	Recommendation: Do pass with amendments to the A-Eng. bill. (Printed B-Eng.)
2-25 (S)	Second reading.
2-26 (S)	Carried over to 02-29 by unanimous consent.
2-29 (S)	Third reading. Carried by Prozanski. Passed. Ayes, 25; nays, 2--Boquist, Girod; excused, 3--Ferrioli, Thomsen, Winters.
2-29 (S)	President Courtney, Riley, Thatcher, excused, granted unanimous consent to vote aye.
3-1 (H)	House concurred in Senate amendments and repassed bill. Ayes, 57; Absent, 1--Boone; Excused, 2--McKeown, Nearman.
3-2 (H)	Speaker signed.
3-4 (S)	President signed.
3-29 (H)	Governor signed.
4-14 (H)	Chapter 72, (2016 Laws): Effective date March 29, 2016.

The bill was assigned to the House Judiciary Committee which held a public hearing on February 8 and a work session on February 10. The bill was also assigned to the Senate Judiciary Committee which held a public hearing on February 22 and a work session on February 23.

For older bills, the Measure History is available in print. Prior to 1997, the series was called *Oregon Legislative Assembly Final Legislative Calendar*, and it is currently called the *Oregon Final Status Report for Legislative Measures*. Each volume lists, in separate sections, Oregon Senate and House bills from a legislative session. The bills are listed in numerical order by bill number. The entry for each bill number is similar to the OLIS Measure History. Note the committee and dates of public hearings and work sessions and note the date of floor activity.

E. Step Five: Look Up the Committee Activity and Bill File

Using the information from the bill's measure history, you can find the committee minutes/logs, recordings and any exhibits. For recent bills on OLIS, the public hearings and work sessions are hyperlinked. Following the links will lead to a committee page that may have an agenda, meeting materials, or a log. To access the recording, look up the date on the right side of the screen and select the play icon next to the date. In the example from Step four (2016 HB 4066), scroll down to 2-10(H) and select "Work Session held." The resulting page shows the details for the House Judiciary's work session on HB 4066. In the right panel, you can select the play icon next to "2/10/2016 3:00 PM" to view the recording.

Also, on the main page for the bill on OLIS, you can select the Text tab for versions of the bill and the Analysis tab for other reports that are part of the bill file.

Committee minutes, audio logs and recordings may also be found on the Oregon State Archives website.[21] It is organized by year then committee name. Committee materials for older legislation can be found on microfilm at Oregon law libraries and at State Archives. With the list of committees and dates from step four, go to the microfilm to find the minutes. The microfilm material is organized by committee, with committee names listed in alphabetical order. Under each committee, the minutes are arranged by date. The exhibits are contained on separate microfilms, arranged by committee and bill number. To listen to the recordings, you must go to the State Archives in Salem or order a copy of the relevant tapes. Some Oregon law libraries will have the text for versions of the bills in print; other analysis or reports are in the bill file in Salem.

---

21. https://sos.oregon.gov/archives/Pages/records/legislative_minutes.aspx.

IV. Tracking Legislation

Of the many bills that are introduced in each legislative session, some may affect the rights of a client by proposing new laws or amending existing laws. In advising a client, an attorney needs to learn of any relevant bills and follow their progress through the legislative process. This skill is called tracking on legislation.

A. Learning about Pending Bills

If you know the number of a bill that you need to track, go to the Oregon Legislative Information System (OLIS). The default is the current session, so if you need to go to a previous session, select the "Session" icon at the top right of the page. Then click the "bills" icon at the top right and enter the bill number. The resulting bill page will have an overview, measure history and scheduled events that you can consult to determine the bill's current statute.

To search for bills on a particular topic, go to OLIS, and in the relevant session, select the "bills" icon, and under the "Bill Text" tab, enter search terms.

B. Finding Pending Legislation That Affects Statutes

Often lawyers wish to know if any new legislation impacts a statute. On Lexis and Westlaw, you can look up the statute, then look for a warning citator symbol. On Lexis, a yellow inverted triangle with an exclamation point indicates pending legislation while Westlaw will have a yellow flag. Selecting the citator symbol will lead you to the bill and tracking information.

On OLIS, go to the relevant session, use the "Today's Publications" dropdown menu to find "Cumulative Session Publications," and select "Statutes Affected by Measures." In the alternative, go to the ORS on the Oregon Legislature's website. In the right panel, navigate to the Statutes Affected by Measures box and select the relevant legislative session.

Chapter 7

Researching Oregon Local Law

CHAPTER GOALS

After reading this chapter, you will be able to

1. Define "home rule" in Oregon;
2. List the types of local governments in Oregon;
3. Demonstrate how to find local government laws; and
4. Identify other sources of local government information.

I. Overview

Local law is the law that governs cities, counties, regions and special districts. Local governments are responsible for a community's basic needs and services, such as sewer and water treatment, police and fire protection, street maintenance, social services, and building permits.

When researching local government laws in Oregon, you will always consult the specific government's website. Further research will depend on the source of the government's power. With home rule governments, research will involve finding a charter, ordinances, and possibly regulations. Otherwise, you should search the ORS and/or the Oregon Constitution for the statutes governing the topic or the "principal act" creating the government. For a more comprehensive discussion of municipal law, consult secondary sources such as the Oregon BarBooks or a local government association website.

This chapter will explain the nature of local government power in Oregon (home rule) and how to research the different types of local governments.

II. Home Rule

In many states, local governments derive their powers from statutes and the state legislature. In Oregon, local voters can adopt charters that define the powers of a city, county, or regional government.[1] These "home rule" charters are similar to a constitution in that they set up the system of government for the community and empower that government to address matters of local concern.[2] For example, a city charter might create a commission or mayor-council form of government, empower that government to pass ordinances, and authorize a municipal court to hear cases involving violations of those ordinances.

There are limits, however, on the powers of home rule cities, counties and regional governments. They are controlled by the Oregon and U.S. Constitutions, and they are preempted by state law. A local law is preempted when the state legislature expressly precludes local regulation or when compliance with both state and local laws is impossible.[3]

Home rule charters do not govern all local governments. Counties also function as agents of the state for some services, and the authority of special districts comes from statutes, not a charter.

III. Types of Local Governments

Researching local government law varies depending on the type of local government and the source of its power. Research usually will involve spending a great deal of time exploring the government's website, consulting the government association's website, and looking at the ORS for an authorizing statute (if applicable) or a preempting statute. (See Table 7.1 for examples.)

---

1. Oregon Constitution, Article XI, section 2.

2. League of Oregon Cities, Local Government: The Basics, *League of Oregon Cities* (2023), https://www.orcities.org/application/files/5416/8184/4848/LocalGovtBasics-3-2023-web.pdf.

3. League of Oregon Cities, *Home Rule 101*, https://www.orcities.org/application/files/4617/1700/1308/Home-Rule-101-updated-8-18-23.pdf; LOC, *Legal guide to Oregon's Statutory Preemptions of Home Rule*, https://www.orcities.org/application/files/9116/9343/3097/Guide-OregonsStatutoryPreemptionsofHome_Rule-Updated8-18-23.pdf; Constitutional Law, Ch. 10 (OSB Legal Pubs 2022).

Table 7.1. Examples of Resources for Types of Local Governments

Type of Local Government	Source of Power	Useful Resources	Examples
City	Charter	City's website, League of Oregon Cities[4]	Portland, Beaverton, Salem, Eugene
County	Statute, Charter, "Home rule" authority	County's website, Association of Oregon Counties[5]	Multnomah, Washington, Marion, Lane
Metropolitan Service District	Statute, Constitution, Charter	Metro's website[6]	Portland Area Metropolitan Service District (Metro)
Special Districts	Statute, Constitution	Special district's website, Special Districts Association of Oregon[7]	Tualatin Valley Fire & Rescue, Siuslaw Public Library District, Sweet Home Cemetery Maintenance District, Tri-County Metropolitan Transportation District (TriMet)
Regional	Agreement between local governments	Regional government's website	Mid-Willamette Valley COG, Rogue Valley COG, Northwest Senior and Disability Services

4. https://www.orcities.org/.
5. https://oregoncounties.org/.
6. https://www.oregonmetro.gov/.
7. https://www.sdao.com/homepage.

A. City Governments

All 242 Oregon cities have a home rule charter. Depending on the charter, the structure of the city government might include an elected mayor and council.

1. Municipal Charter and Code

The council might pass laws (ordinances) and adopt resolutions. The ordinances are compiled by subject in a municipal code. The best place to find the charter and code is the city's website. The city's website will also have maps and various policy documents, but the searching can be cumbersome. Lexis has a limited number of municipal codes, and although there are various platforms that host codes, their websites do not tend to offer strong searching or navigation tools. Table 7.2 lists where to find municipal codes.

Table 7.2. Locating Municipal Codes

City Website (example: https://www.eugene-or.gov)
Lexis: Select "state" then Oregon. In Statutes and Legislation, select Oregon Municipal Codes
Municode: https://library.municode.com/or
eCode360: https://www.generalcode.com/library/#OR
American Legal Publishing: https://codelibrary.amlegal.com/regions/or

2. Municipal Courts

A city charter or ordinance may also create a municipal court.[8] These courts must hear misdemeanors created by the charter or ordinances and traffic crimes under ORS 801.545. Depending on the charter or ordinance, the courts may hear other misdemeanors committed or triable in the city except certain drug-related misdemeanors.[9] Municipal court decisions can be appealed to the circuit court for the county or the Oregon Court of Appeals, depending on the circumstances.[10]

8. Oregon Constitution Art. VII, sec. 1.

9. League of Oregon Cities, Oregon Municipal Handbook, Chapter 6 Municipal Courts https://www.orcities.org/resources/guides-handbooks/city-handbook.

10. *Id.*

Instead of creating a municipal court system, some cities will form an agreement with the justice court of the local county circuit court. In cities with a population over 300,000, the county circuit court must act as the municipal court.[11] Portland is the only city that falls within this category.

3. League of Oregon Cities

A good source for information on Oregon municipal law is the League of Oregon Cities (LOC). The LOC was created through an intergovernmental agreement between the cities in 1925.[12] It provides advocacy support and information to cities, including guides, handbooks and other reference materials. The *Oregon Municipal Handbook* is a particularly comprehensive resource on municipal governance.[13]

B. County Government

Oregon counties are hybrid governments: they are both an agent of the state and have "home rule" authority. The state legislature creates counties, designates their boundaries and delegates various powers to counties. In addition to their state powers, counties also have "home rule" authority either through a charter or chapter 203 of the *Oregon Revised Statutes.*

Counties may be governed by a board of commissioners or a "county court" (a county judge and two commissioners). The county code, ordinances, and charter (if the county has a charter) can be found on the county's webpage. Researchers also should look for the relevant department on the county's website and search the entire site for their topic to find any other relevant information.

Because counties are an administrative division of the state, researchers also should consult the *Oregon Revised Statutes* and the relevant state department's website. For example, the county justice court is on the county's website, but the county circuit court is on the Oregon Judicial Branch's website. Either court might hear cases involving state law traffic violations.

---

11. ORS 3.136.

12. League of Oregon Cities : Governing Documents, https://www.orcities.org/about/how-we-work/governing-guidelines.

13. League of Oregon Cities, *supra* note 8.

When researching Oregon county governance, a useful source of information is the Association of Oregon Counties (AOC).[14] This organization provides advocacy and information for Oregon counties.

C. Metropolitan Areas

Metropolitan areas can form districts to provide public services under chapter 268 of the *Oregon Revised Statutes*. Voters of such a district can also adopt a home rule charter under the Oregon Constitution, Art. XI, sec. 14. The only metropolitan service district that has been formed is the Portland Area Metropolitan Service District (Metro). It covers the twenty-five cities within Clackamas, Multnomah and Washington counties. Some of its responsibilities include sewage, the zoo, transportation and land use planning. These duties, powers, and responsibilities are defined by its charter, ORS chapter 268 and the Oregon Constitution, so researchers should consult all these sources. The Metro Charter, Code, and administrative rules can be found on Metro's website in the "About Metro" section.[15] Also, the "Library" section of the website provides a wealth of materials including, plans, studies, maps, and other publications.[16]

D. Special Districts

Special service districts provide a particular purpose to a particular region. There are over 1000 special districts in Oregon, covering twenty-eight types of services, such as rural fire, mass transit, hospital, and cemetery maintenance districts.

Unlike previously discussed types of local governments, special districts derive their authority from statute—not home rule charter. Chapter 198 of the ORS governs special districts generally, and the ORS section that covers the particular type of district is called the "principal act." The principal act will define the district's duties, limits on its authority, and methods of elections. The principal act typically gives the district power to sue and be sued, enter into contracts and levy taxes. Therefore, a researcher must consult the principal act. The Oregon Constitution also provides for the formation of some special districts, such as public utilities, so it should also be checked.[17]

14. https://oregoncounties.org/.
15. https://www.oregonmetro.gov/how-metro-works/metro-code.
16. https://www.oregonmetro.gov/library.
17. Art. XI, sec. 12.

Other useful sources for information include the district's website and the website of the Special Districts Association of Oregon (SDAO).[18] The SDAO provides advocacy and support for its special district members. On their website, the SDAO Resource Links page provides useful links organized by type of district,[19] and the SDAO Administrative Manual explains the process of forming a district.[20] To learn more about special districts and their relationship to cities and counties, see Chapter 11 of the *Oregon Municipal Handbook*.

E. Regional Governments

Local governments can create associations that coordinate on regional planning and development issues. These associations are typically referred to as regional governments or councils of governments (COGS). The *Oregon Bluebook* provides contact information and a link to the website for the six regional governments in Oregon.[21]

When researching an issue involving a regional government, you should consider consulting:

- Regional government's website,
- Chapter 190 of the ORS which authorizes these associations, and
- Land Use, Oregon BarBooks, Chapter 7: Regional Planning.

18. *Supra* note 7.
19. https://www.sdao.com/resource-links.
20. https://www.sdao.com/publications.
21. League of Oregon Cities, *supra* note 8.

Chapter 8

Researching Oregon Administrative Law

CHAPTER GOALS

After reading this chapter, you will be able to

1. List the sources of and constraints on agency power;
2. Demonstrate how to find agency regulations;
3. Describe methods for locating agency decisions; and
4. Identify ways to find other agency materials and information.

Administrative law is the law produced by the executive/administrative branch. This branch is charged with executing the laws, so agencies within this branch might create rules that provide specific details to statutes, issue licenses permitting individuals or businesses to take certain actions, conduct investigations to see whether rules are being followed, and decide cases where the application of rules or denial of a license is at issue. Agencies are involved in a myriad of topics from environmental programs to massage therapist licenses to requirements for in-state tuition at Oregon universities. Therefore, Oregon lawyers frequently interact with state agencies.

The first part of this chapter introduces administrative agencies and their functions. The next part explains how to research administrative law in Oregon.

I. Understanding Oregon Agencies

Agencies are administered by the executive branch. While the chief executive power is vested in the governor, there are four other elected positions that may also manage agencies: the secretary of state, treasurer, attorney general, and commissioner of labor and industries. The terminology for agencies is inconsistent — they may be called boards, commissions and departments. To make sense of the system, this section explores how to find relevant agencies, determine their source power, and identify their functions and oversight.

A. Finding Oregon Agencies

Table 8.1. How to Find Agencies

1.	Enabling statute or Constitution provision creating the agency
2.	Chapter 182 of the ORS
3.	Oregon Bluebook

Governmental agencies in Oregon may include boards, commissions, and departments—the terminology is inconsistent. They are created by statute, so the primary way to find an agency is through the course of researching statutes. Within a relevant statute, there will be a section that delegates powers to an agency. These sections are called enabling statutes.

In addition to the enabling statute, chapter 182 of the *Oregon Revised Statutes* (ORS) lists the agencies found in Oregon. Another helpful source for finding agencies is the *Oregon Bluebook*. It lists state agencies and provides a short description for each. From the home page, select "State Agencies A-Z." Table 8.1 summarizes how to find agencies in Oregon.

B. Sources of Agency Authority

Table 8.2. Sources of Agency Authority

1.	Enabling statute
2.	Constitutional provision
3.	Oregon Administrative Procedure Act

Agencies are created by the legislature through an enabling statute or by the state constitution through the initiative process. The statutory or constitutional provisions that create agencies establish the powers and duties of the agencies. Each agency must work within the limits set by these provisions.

In general, agencies also must operate within the bounds of the Oregon Administrative Procedure Act (APA), found in chapter 183 of the ORS. The APA requires that the public be involved in developing agency policy and drafting rules. The APA also sets requirements for administrative hearings to ensure they are conducted fairly. Table 8.2 lists sources of agency authority.

C. Types of Agency Functions

The functions of an agency are set forth in the enabling statute or the constitutional provision that created the agency. Agencies perform the functions of all three branches of government.

Table 8.3. Agency Functions

Legislative	• Promulgate rules (regulations)
Executive	• Issue licenses and permits • Discipline licensees/permittees (suspend, revoke, reprimand, sanction) • Impose civil penalties • Issue cease-and-desist orders
Judicial	• Adjudicate disputes

Agencies promulgate rules (also called regulations) interpreting the statutes that they administer. These rules are similar in form and in authority to statutes enacted by the legislature but are much more detailed. They are published by the Secretary of State in the *Oregon Administrative Rules Compilation* (OAR).

The main functions of most agencies concern their executive powers—administering laws. Agencies issue licenses which are defined as "any agency permit, certificate, approval, registration or similar form of permission required by law to pursue any commercial activity, trade, occupation or profession."[1] They might discipline a licensee's violations of the agency's statute or rules. When non-licensees engage in prohibited conduct, agencies may have the power to issue cease-and-desist orders and/or impose civil penalties (i.e., monetary penalties).

Agencies also have quasi-judicial functions. In order to enforce laws, they may have to make decisions on individual cases that that involve the agency's rules or its mission (e.g., to suspend a dental license or award unemployment benefits). They may hold hearings that are less formal and complicated than court proceedings. Although agencies do not have the power to criminally fine

1. ORS 183.310(5).

or imprison, they can investigate and initiate prosecutions. Table 8.3 provides a summary of agency functions.

D. Agency Oversight

Each of the three branches of government has some oversight of agency functions. The legislative branch generally grants agencies the power to perform their duties and provides funding for the agency to operate. The courts may review an agency decision or determine in contested cases whether an agency's rules are valid. The governor is the supervisor of all executive agencies, and the executive branch appoints some agencies' highest officials.

II. Researching Oregon Administrative Law

Oregon administrative law research has six essential steps (see Table 8.4).

Table 8.4. Researching Administrative Law

1. Find the enabling statute
2. Locate the rules in the OAR
3. Update the rule and find proposed changes
4. Find agency and judicial decisions applying the rules
5. Consult agency website for other materials
6. Look for Attorney General Opinions or other guidance

A. Find the Enabling Statute

The first step in administrative law research is to find the enabling statute, i.e., the statute that gives the agency its power. The enabling statute will define the powers and functions of the agency. Chapter 5 explains the process of researching statutes.

Sometimes, instead of an enabling statute, a constitutional provision will create an agency and establish its powers and duties. Even in these situations, it is important to research the ORS to determine if there are related statutes.

For example, the State Lottery Commission was created through the initiative process that amended the Oregon Constitution, and following the passage of that amendment, the legislature enacted ORS chapter 461 to implement it. Researching constitutional provisions is covered in Chapter 4.

B. Locate the Rules in the OAR

If the legislature delegated to an agency the power to create rules, the next step is to locate those rules. This section explains what administrative rules are, how they are published, where they are found, and how to read them.

1. What Are Administrative Rules?

Administrative rules provide more details to general statutes since agencies are experts in particular areas. Rules may provide guidance based on an agency's understanding of a relevant statute and/or state procedures for agency activities like issuing licenses, inspecting facilities, etc. Although rules are primary authority, they are subordinate to statutes.

If there is any inconsistency between a rule and a statute, the statute wins. Moreover, a rule cannot "cure" or fix a statute that a court has held to be unconstitutional.

2. OAR Organization and Citation

Administrative rules in Oregon are published by the Oregon Secretary of State in *Oregon Administrative Rules Compilation* (OAR). They are organized by agency then subject then individual rule. Citations to rules contain the abbreviation "OAR" followed by a ten-digit number in the form 000-000-0000. The first three digits identify the agency's chapter number (each agency is assigned a chapter number; the chapter number is not related at all to chapters of ORS or *Oregon Laws*). The next three digits are a division number, which groups related rules together. The last four digits represent the number assigned to a particular rule. Table 8.5 show an example of this numbering.

Table 8.5. Oregon Administrative Rules Numbering

The rules of the Board of Massage Therapists are contained in chapter 334 of *Oregon Administrative Rules Compilation*. Chapter 334 is separated into five divisions:

Division 1: Procedural Rules

Division 10: Massage Licensing

Division 20: Sanitation, Facility and Building Requirements

Division 30: Ethical Standards

Division 40: Complaints and Discipline

Within division 10, OAR 334-010-0005 contains rules for applying to take the exam to be licensed as a massage therapist; it requires certain forms to be submitted with the required fee, a copy of photo identification, class transcripts, etc. A later rule in that division, OAR 334-010-0012, sets out the appeal procedures for an applicant who fails the examination.

3. Location of OAR

Once you determine the agency through the enabling act or the constitutional provision, go to the OAR and look up the agency's chapter number. The OAR is available on the Oregon Secretary of State's website, Westlaw and Lexis (see Table 8.6). These sources allow users to browse, search by rule number and search by terms.

Table 8.6. Location of Oregon Administrative Rules Compilation

<table>
<tr><td rowspan="3">OARD
Secretary of State's website[2]
(free and official)</td><td>Browse:
1. Select Browse by Chapter
2. Click on Chapter Name radio button
3. Use "Select a chapter..." dropdown menu to find agency name
4. Select the relevant division then rule number</td></tr>
<tr><td>Search by Rule:
1. Select Quick Search By Rule Number
2. Enter ten-digit number in the search box</td></tr>
<tr><td>Search by Term:
1. Select Rule Text Search
2. Use the "Select a Chapter..." dropdown to find the agency
3. Enter search terms in the "Search By" boxes</td></tr>
<tr><td>Lexis</td><td>State > Oregon > OR–Oregon Administrative Rules</td></tr>
<tr><td>Westlaw</td><td>State Materials > Oregon > Oregon Regulations</td></tr>
</table>

The Oregon Secretary of State's website provides the OAR through the Oregon Administrative Rules Database (OARD). This database is free, updated as soon as rules are received and approved, and easy to use.

Oregon administrative rules are also available on both Lexis and Westlaw. Although they are not always as current as the OARD, their citator functions, Shepard's (Lexis) and KeyCite (Westlaw), can be very useful for finding cases (see subsection D).

2. https://secure.sos.state.or.us/oard/ruleSearch.action.

4. Reading the Rules

After finding relevant rules, read the text of each rule carefully. Many techniques used for reading statutes apply equally well to reading administrative rules. These techniques are discussed in Chapter 5, Section II. B. In particular, always look for a separate rule that provides definitions, be aware of cross references, read the text several times, and outline any complicated provisions.

C. Update the Rule and Find Proposed Changes

Updating ensures that you have the current version of the rule and that you know about any recent proposed changes. The OARD is always current since it is updated continuously as rules are filed and approved. On Westlaw and Lexis there will be information on the currentness of the rule directly under the rule title. If it is not today's date, look up the rule in the OARD.

To find any proposed changes, consult the *Oregon Bulletin*. This monthly publication provides notice of proposed action on rules by various agencies. It also provides the text of new rules, executive orders and other helpful material. The easiest method to access any proposed changes to a rule is to use the citators on Westlaw and Lexis. In the alternative, one can access the *Oregon Bulletin* through the OARD. Table 8.7 summarizes locating proposed changes to the rules.

Table 8.7. Locating Proposed Changes to Rules

Oregon Bulletin, OARD[3]	1. Select the year then month 2. Under "Notices of Proposed Rulemaking," select Agency to list by agency 3. Locate agency, then use the caption to determine if there are prosed rules
Lexis	1. Go to rule 2. In the right panel, under Related Content, select Find references to this administrative code
Westlaw	1. Go to rule 2. Select flag next to rule number

3. https://secure.sos.state.or.us/oard/displayBulletins.action.

D. Find Agency and Judicial Decisions

Table 8.8. Locating Agency Decisions

1. Check agency's website
2. Use citator on Westlaw for the rule
3. Westlaw's Oregon Administrative Decisions & Guidance collection
4. Lexis's All Oregon Administrative Materials collection
5. Fastcase

In addition to their rulemaking function, agencies act in a quasi-judicial role, adjudicating cases pertaining to agency rules or actions. There may be several levels of agency review, depending on the agency. Check with a particular agency to learn the procedure it follows. The first level may involve a reviewer or adjudicator considering the claimant's file and making a recommendation or determination. Subsequently, a hearing may be held before an Administrative Law Judge (ALJ).[4] These proceedings may resemble short, informal trials, and afterwards, the ALJ may issue a final order or proposed order. That order may be reviewed by the agency which will issue a final order.[5]

Some agency orders are widely available, while others are more difficult to locate. Some may be available only from the agency itself. Table. 8.8. shows locations for agency orders.

1. Agency Websites

Orders from some agencies may be available on the deciding agency's website. When exploring the agency's website, note that the agency might call their decisions "orders," "opinions," or "sanctions." Some agencies, such as the Oregon State Bar Disciplinary Board, collect their decisions in reporters (i.e., *Disciplinary Board Reporter*). If you are unable to find the agency's decisions,

4. Most Oregon agencies are required to use ALJs from the Office of Administrative Hearings (OAH). For more information, see Oregon Administrative Law (OSB Legal Pubs 2010) and the OAH website at www.oregon.gov/oah. Note that ALJs are not required to be attorneys.

5. The final order should contain information about appeals. Administrative orders may be appealed to an appeals board at the agency, circuit court, the Tax Court or the Oregon Court of Appeals. Oregon courts have jurisdiction to review both the validity of agency rules and final orders, ORS 183.400, 183.480, so conducting case research may reveal cases that address the agency rules and orders relevant to your research. Case research is covered in Chapter 9.

contact the agency. It's possible that the decisions are available only from the agency.

2. Lexis and Westlaw

Lexis and Westlaw provide access to decisions and guidance for certain agencies such as Oregon Bureau of Labor & Industry, Oregon Environmental Quality Commission, Oregon Land Use Board of Appeals (LUBA), and the Oregon Public Utility Commission.

A convenient way to access these decisions is through Westlaw's citator. When viewing a rule on Westlaw, select the Citing References tab then Administrative Decisions and Guidance. You can select the filters in the left column to search for terms or narrow the results by date.

3. Fastcase

Fastcase has decisions from the Liquor Control Commission, Worker's Compensation Board and various health care boards. To access the decisions, select Browse Libraries from the homepage. If you are not automatically taken to Oregon & Federal materials, type Oregon into the "Change jurisdiction by typing" box in the upper left corner of the page. To only view Oregon materials, deselect "Include related federal" in the upper right corner of the page. The Administrative Materials contains a list of agencies. After you select an agency, enter your search terms.

E. Consult Agency Websites

In addition to rules and agency decisions, you should consult useful secondary sources. A large part of your research should be exploring the agency's website for guidance. Also, Oregon Attorney General opinions might provide advice on your issue, and sometimes an administrative law manual or treatise can be quite useful.

The most valuable resource in administrative law research is often the agency itself. An agency might have secondary sources that are very useful such as policies, guidelines, manuals, instructions and forms. All Oregon agencies are linked from the state's website at www.oregon.gov. Consider searching the site for your topic to see if other agencies provide guidance. Also, consider talking to the agency's representatives to find out what material is available. Either go to the "about" section of the agency's website or consult the Secretary of State's "State Agency Rules Coordinator Contact List," which provides the name and phone number for a contact person in each agency.[6]

F. Find Attorney General Opinions

As the state's lawyer, the Attorney General provides opinions to the state that are similar to the advice of an attorney to a client. The opinions respond to specific questions posed by the Governor, an agency official, or a legislator. These opinions are advisory—not mandatory—orders; however, they are considered strongly persuasive.

There are two categories of opinions, formal and informal (see Table 8.9).

Table 8.9. Comparison of Formal and Informal Opinions

	Formal	Informal
Type of question	Constitutional issues and matters of statewide concern	Specific to the party requesting the opinion
Designation	Four-digit number (OP 8295)	Year, dash, number (OP 2018-1)
Signature	Signed by Attorney General	Signed by Chief Counsel of the Department of Justice General Counsel Division

Opinions were first compiled and published in bound volumes called *Opinions of the Attorney General of the State of Oregon*, but since 1997, they have been released individually. Although the print version can be found in libraries and digitized online by HeinOnline, the best source for finding current opinions is the Oregon Department of Justice website. Table 8.10 provides the sources for finding these opinions.

6. https://sos.oregon.gov/archives/Pages/rules-coordinator-contact.aspx.

Table 8.10. Sources of Attorney General Opinions

Source	Location	Coverage	Finding Aids
Oregon Department of Justice website[7]	Attorney General heading > Office of the Attorney General (subheading) > Attorney General Opinions (left panel)	1997–current	Keyword search
HeinOnline	State Attorney General Reports and Opinions	1901–2022	Keyword search; indexes
Lexis	All Oregon Administrative Materials	1920–current	Keyword search
Westlaw	Oregon Administrative Decisions and Guidance	1920–current	Keyword search
Opinions of the Attorney General of the State of Oregon[8] (print)	State law libraries; Department of Justice (fee required)	1901–1997	Indexes

7. https://www.doj.state.or.us/oregon-department-of-justice/office-of-the-attorney-general/attorney-general-opinions/.

8. Publication of the *Opinions of the Attorney General of the State of Oregon* began in 1901 and includes indexes. These are cited by volume and page number. This publication stopped in 1997. Although many Oregon law libraries have this print version, it has also been digitized by HeinOnline.

Chapter 9

Researching Oregon Court Opinions

CHAPTER GOALS

After reading this chapter, you will be able to

1. Identify and explain the court structure in Oregon;
2. Identify and explain the parts of a reported cases;
3. Use research strategies to find cases; and
4. Read and analyze cases effectively.

A judicial opinion, also called a case, is written by a court to explain its decision in a dispute. Cases are available online on court websites, free sources like Google Scholar, and commercial sites including Lexis and Westlaw. In print, cases are published in rough chronological order in books called *reporters*. Even researchers working solely with online resources must be familiar with reporters because case citation formats and pagination are still based on print reporters. This chapter begins with an overview of the Oregon court system. Then it explains reporters and online sources used to locate Oregon cases when you have a citation. Next, the chapter outlines the anatomy of a case. After that introduction of the context and structure of cases, the chapter explains multiple strategies for finding cases, as well as updating case law research. The last part of the chapter discusses strategic reading of cases, which is a crucial part of an accurate and thorough research process.

I. Oregon Courts

Table 9.1. Basic Court Structure

Court Type	Name of Oregon Court
Trial	Oregon Circuit Court
Intermediate Court of Appeals	Oregon Court of Appeals
Ultimate Appellate Court	Oregon Supreme Court
Tax (trial)	Oregon Tax Court

In the Oregon state system, the trial courts of general jurisdiction are called *circuit courts*. These courts exist in each of Oregon's thirty-six counties; some counties are combined to create Oregon's twenty-seven judicial districts. To demonstrate, Lane County is the only county in the Second Judicial District, which has fifteen circuit judges. These judges hear cases only from Lane County. The Seventh Judicial District includes five counties (Hood River, Wasco, Sherman, Wheeler, and Gilliam) and has four circuit judges, who hear cases from any of those five counties.

In addition to the circuit courts, the Oregon Tax Court serves as the trial court for all state cases in which Oregon tax law is at issue. Take care not to confuse the state circuit courts, which are trial courts, with the federal circuit courts, which are appellate courts.

Oregon's intermediate court is called the Court of Appeals. Located in Salem, the Court of Appeals is composed of thirteen elected judges. Cases decided by this intermediate court of appeals are heard by three judges sitting as a *panel* of the full court; the chief judge acts as a substitute when needed.

The Supreme Court of Oregon is the court of last resort. It also sits primarily in Salem and has seven elected justices. The seven justices sit together, called *en banc*, to hear all cases. Table 9.1 details the basic court structure.

The Oregon Judicial Department website contains the following useful information:

- An explanation of state court jurisdiction,
- A map of circuit courts in Oregon,
- Links to state courts' websites,
- Directory of court personnel,

- Court-approved forms, and
- Recent appellate court opinions.

II. Sources for Oregon Cases

Oregon cases are available online and in print. Even though you will conduct most of your case research online, you will often find cases by reference to the volume and page number where those cases appear in print reporters. This part of the chapter introduces official reporters, commercially produced regional reporters, and online sources for Oregon cases.

A. Official Reporters for Oregon Cases

Table 9.2. Reporters for Oregon cases

Reporter	Court	Example Citation
Oregon Reports	Oregon Supreme Court	*Owen v. City of Portland*, 367 Or 661 (2021).[1]
Oregon Reports, Court of Appeals	Oregon Appellate Court	*State v. Hart*, 222 Or App 285 (2008).
Oregon Tax Reports	Oregon Tax Court	*Comcast Corp. v. Dept. of Revenue*, 22 OTR 442 (2017).
West's *Pacific Reporter*	Oregon Appellate Courts (along with 14 other state appellate courts)	*Owen v. City of Portland*, 497 P.3d 1216 (Or. 2021).

1. Under the Oregon courts' citation rules, no periods are used in reporter abbreviations. This rule differs from other states' citation rules and from the national citation systems. See Appendix A for a discussion of citation rules. Outside of Oregon, the citation for the *Owen* case would be 367 Or. 661 (2021). In either citation system, the reporter identifies which court decided the case, as only Oregon Supreme Court cases are published in Or and only Oregon Court of Appeals cases are published in Or App.

Oregon Reports and *Oregon Reports, Court of Appeals* are the *official reporters*[2] for Oregon appellate cases. All cases decided by the Oregon Supreme Court are published in *Oregon Reports*. The abbreviation for this reporter is "Or" (though some online services use "Ore" to distinguish the word "or" in searches). The case of *Owen v. City of Portland* can be found in volume 367 of the series *Oregon Reports*, starting on page 661. The case was decided in 2021.

Oregon's intermediate appellate court opinions are published in a separate reporter called *Oregon Reports, Court of Appeals*. "Or App" is the abbreviation for this reporter. The case *State v. Hart* was published in volume 222 of the reporter series *Oregon Reports, Court of Appeals*, beginning on page 285. It was decided in 2008. Almost all opinions of the Court of Appeals are published.[3] Citations to Oregon cases include the case name, the reporter volume and abbreviation, the first page of the case, and the date.

Cases from the State of Oregon trial courts are not published but may be obtained directly from the court that decided the case, as well as online. Oregon tax court decisions are reported in *Oregon Tax Reports*, abbreviated "OTR" in Oregon, or "Or. Tax" outside of Oregon.

B. Regional Reporters and Oregon Cases

Cases from Oregon appellate courts are also reported in a commercially produced regional reporter called West's *Pacific Reporter*. While the text of the court's opinion is the same in the official and unofficial reporters, the appearance, pagination, and editorial research aids may be different. Because Oregon courts cite to the official reporters, lawyers submitting briefs to those courts often cite the official reporters, too, but lawyers in other states are most likely to cite to the regional reporter for Oregon cases.

West's Pacific Reporter publishes appellate cases from the courts of fifteen states: Alaska, Arizona, California, Colorado, Hawaii, Idaho, Kansas, Montana, Nevada, New Mexico, Oklahoma, Oregon, Utah, Washington, and Wyo-

2. An official reporter is the government-approved publication. When drafting a document for the court, the official reporter should be cited.

3. Sometimes the Court of Appeals affirms a case without writing an opinion. These cases are "affirmed without opinion," sometimes referred to as "AWOPs." They are listed in a table of Oregon Reports, Court of Appeals, and on the court's website, but should not be cited.

ming. It is one of seven regional reporters[4] that publish state appellate cases. West decided which states' cases to publish together in its regional reporters, so these groupings have no legal impact.[5]

When a reporter reaches a certain volume number, the publisher begins another series. In 1931, after publishing volume 300 of *Pacific Reporter*, West began again with volume one of *Pacific Reporter, Second Series*. In 2000, following publication of volume 999 in the second series, West started a third series, *Pacific Reporter, Third Series*. To find a case in a reporter with multiple series, you must know which series the case was reported in.

To indicate which state's courts decided the cases included in a regional reporter, a citation includes an abbreviation at the beginning of the date parenthetical. (Note that the following examples use the national citation format of using periods in reporter abbreviations.)

> Examples: *Owen v. City of Portland*, 497 P.3d 1216 (Or. 2021). *State v. Hart*, 193 P.3d 42 (Or. App. 2008).

If you are not sure which reporter a reader may prefer, you may want to include citations to both reporters. Two citations that refer to the same case in different reporters are called *parallel citations*.

---

4. West's Regional reporters: *Atlantic Reporter* (A., A.2d, A.3d): Connecticut, Delaware, District of Columbia, Maine, Maryland, New Hampshire, New Jersey, Pennsylvania, Rhode Island, and Vermont; *North Eastern Reporter* (N.E., N.E.2d, N.E.3d): Illinois, Indiana, Massachusetts, New York, and Ohio; *North Western Reporter* (N.W., N.W.2d): Iowa, Michigan, Minnesota, Nebraska, North Dakota, South Dakota, and Wisconsin; *Pacific Reporter* (P., P.2d, P.3d): Alaska, Arizona, California, Colorado, Hawaii, Idaho, Kansas, Montana, Nevada, New Mexico, Oklahoma, Oregon, Utah, Washington, and Wyoming; *Southern Reporter* (So., So. 2d, So. 3d): Alabama, Florida, Louisiana, and Mississippi; *South Eastern Reporter* (S.E., S.E.2d): Georgia, North Carolina, South Carolina, Virginia, and West Virginia; *South Western Reporter* (S.W., S.W.2d, S.W.3d): Arkansas, Kentucky, Missouri, Tennessee, and Texas.

5. Note that the coverage of each regional reporter is **not the same** as the composition of the federal circuits. The federal Ninth Circuit includes Alaska, Arizona, California, Hawaii, Idaho, Montana, Nevada, Oregon, and Washington, as well as Guam and the Northern Mariana Islands. It does not include Colorado, Kansas, New Mexico, Oklahoma, Utah, or Wyoming, yet those states' cases are reported in *Pacific Reporter*.

Examples: *Owen v. City of Portland*, 497 P.3d 1216, 367 Or. 661 (2021). *State v. Hart*, 193 P.3d 42, 222 Or. App. 285 (2008).

III. Online Sources for Oregon Cases

A. Free Sources

Oregon cases are available on commercial (paid subscription) platforms and free websites (see Table 9.3). The number of freely available sources of case law has increased over the last few years, and probably will continue to do so. On many of the free sites, date coverage is limited.

Table 9.3. Free Sources for Case Law

Source	Coverage
Caselaw Access Project	Oregon Supreme Court Decisions (1847–2017) Oregon Appellate Court Decisions (1969–2017) Oregon Tax Decisions (1962–2006)
Oregon Judicial Department Website	Oregon Supreme Court (Advance Sheets) Oregon Appellate Court (Advance Sheets) Oregon Tax Court (Advance Sheets) Links to State of Oregon Law Library Digital Collection
State of Oregon Law Library Digital Collection	Oregon Supreme Court Opinions (1998–present) Oregon Court of Appeals Opinions (1998–present) Oregon Tax Court Decisions and Orders
Google Scholar	Oregon appellate and supreme court published cases (1950–present)
Fastcase (Free for Oregon Bar Members)	Oregon Supreme Court Opinions (1938–present) Oregon Court of Appeals Opinions (1969–present) Oregon Tax Court Decisions
Findlaw	Oregon Court of Appeals Decisions (1990–present) Oregon Supreme Court Decisions (1997–present)
Justia	Oregon Supreme Court Decisions (1949–present) Oregon Court of Appeals Decisions (1969–present)

CourtListener	Variable and not comprehensive Oregon Supreme Court Decisions (1848–present) Oregon Appellate Court Decisions (1969–present) Oregon Tax Court (2011–present)

B. Commercial Sources

You are probably familiar with the commercial subscription legal research platforms, which have much more consistent and broad coverage than free platforms. Table 9.4 lists these platforms.

Table 9.4. Subscription Platforms

Platform	Case Law Coverage
Lexis	Oregon Supreme Court Decisions (1847–present) Oregon Appellate Court Decisions (1969–present) Oregon Tax Court Decisions (1962–present)
Westlaw	Oregon Supreme Court Decisions (1853–present) Oregon Appellate Court Decisions (1969–present) Oregon Tax Court Decisions (1962–present)
Bloomberg	Oregon Supreme Court Decisions (1853–present) Oregon Court of Appeals Decisions (1969–present) Oregon Tax Court Decisions (1962–present)

C. Pagination

When working with cases from any online provider, be aware of pagination markers. In addition to providing the first page of a case, information from the case must be cited to a specific page in the print reporter. To show where a page change occurs, online services use *star paging*. Whenever text in the print reporter runs to the next page, that page number will be embedded in the text of the online version and preceded by an asterisk or "star." To give star pagination for multiple reporters, an online provider may assign a different number of asterisks to each reporter (e.g., the star paging for the first full cite given at the top of the screen will have one asterisk, and the star paging for the second will have two asterisks). Whenever a certain reporter changes pages, the new page number will follow the related number of stars. Text following that marker appears on the next page in the reporter. Note that some of the more advanced online services allow you to select which reporter's pagination you want to have indicated, and then show only those pages. You might also sometimes see the page numbers for the selected reporter presented in brackets, without asterisks.

IV. Anatomy of a Reported Case

Each reported case contains the exact language of the court's opinion, but the publisher also provides supplemental information intended to aid researchers in learning about the case, locating the relevant parts of the case, and finding similar cases. Some of these research aids are gathered from the court record of the case, while others are written by the publisher's editorial staff. The following discussion explains the information and enhancements for a published case by referring to the following example from the Oregon Court of Appeals: *State v. Hart*. Most online resources and print reporters will include most of this information and similar enhancements, although perhaps in a different order. Figure 9.1 shows these enhancements.

Figure 9-1. Case Excerpt in Official Reporter

Dates → Submitted October 31, 2007, affirmed September 10, 2008

Parties and procedural designations → STATE OF OREGON,
Plaintiff-Respondent,
v.
PAMELA ANN HART,
Defendant-Appellant.

Washington County Circuit Court

Docket numbers → D055175M; A130811

Parallel cite → 193 P3d 42

Background → **Background:** Defendant was convicted in the Circuit Court, Washington County, Donald R. Letourneau, J., of fourth-degree assault. Defendant appealed.

Holding → **Holding:** The Court of Appeals, Rosenblum, J. held that evidence was sufficient to support conviction.

Disposition → Affirmed.

Headnotes →

1. Criminal Law — Review — Scope of Review in General — Nature of Decision Appealed from as Affecting Scope of Review — In General — Criminal Law — Review — Presumptions — Facts or Proceedings Not Shown by Record — Sufficiency of Evidence — Inferences or Deductions from Evidence.

Court of Appeals reviews the denial of a motion for judgment of acquittal to determine whether the record contains evidence from which a rational trier of fact, drawing all reasonable inferences in the light most favorable to the state, could find all elements of the charged crime beyond a reasonable doubt.

2. Assault and Battery — Criminal Responsibility — Prosecution — Weight and Sufficiency of Evidence — Assault Causing, or Intended to Cause, Great Bodily Harm.

Assuming that rational factfinder could have determined that assault victim suffered substantial pain, as element of charged offense, such determination could not serve as basis for appellate affirmance of defendant's conviction, where factfinder clearly found that there was no evidence that victim suffered substantial pain. ORS 161.015(7).

3. Assault and Battery — Criminal Responsibility — Prosecution — Weight and Sufficiency of Evidence — Assault Causing, or Intended to Cause, Great Bodily Harm.

Evidence that victim sustained half-inch cut to the back of his head, which was still bleeding when police arrived, and was advised by medical personnel to go to the hospital, was sufficient to support finding that victim suffered "impairment of physical condition," as element of fourth-degree assault, as injury interfered with body's ability to function in normal manner by protecting inner body from infection. ORS 161.015(7).

Trial judge → Donald R. Letourneau, Judge.

Attorneys → Peter Ozanne, Executive Director, Peter Gartlan, Chief Defender, Legal Services Division, and Kristin Carveth,

Source: *Oregon Reports, Court of Appeals.*

A. Dates

Reporters typically provide the date the case was argued and submitted to the court, and the date of the court's decision. In *State v. Hart*, the case was submitted on October 31, 2007, and the court issued its decision on September 10, 2008. For most citation purposes, only the year a published case was decided is important.

B. Parties and Procedural Designations

The parties are listed with their procedural designations. In general, if a losing party has a right to appeal, she will be called the *appellant* and the opposing party will be called the *respondent*. If the losing party must ask the court to review the case, he is the *petitioner* and the opposing party will be the *respondent*. The *State v. Hart* case shows that the State of Oregon was the plaintiff but is now the respondent. Pamela Ann Hart was the defendant and is now the appellant.

C. Docket Numbers

The tracking number assigned to the case by a court is called a docket number. Each court assigns a different docket number to the case, just as colleges and universities assign each student a different student identification number. In Oregon, the circuit court docket numbers begin with CC; Court of Appeals docket numbers begin with CA; and Supreme Court docket numbers begin with SC.

Docket numbers are helpful in locating the parties' briefs, a court's orders, or other documents related to that case. Because some of these documents are not published, they can be obtained only from the court that decided the case. To request these documents, you must have the appropriate docket number or, in some instances, the parties' names.

D. Parallel Citations

Cases are often published in multiple reporters or online databases. The citations to these various sources for the same case are *parallel citations*. The parallel citations for the *State v. Hart* decision from the Oregon Court of Appeals are 222 Or App 285 and 193 P3d 42.

E. Synopsis

One of the most helpful research aids included by a publisher's editorial staff is a brief summary of the case; it may be called a synopsis, background, syllabus, or overview. It quickly summarizes the key facts, procedural posture, legal points, and disposition of the case. Reading a synopsis can quickly show whether a case is on point for your research issue. You cannot rely exclusively on a synopsis and must never cite the synopsis, even when it gives an excellent summary of the case.

F. Headnotes

A *headnote* is a sentence or short paragraph that sets out a single point of law in a case. Most cases will have several headnotes because most cases discuss several points of law. The number of headnotes varies by publisher, meaning the number of headnotes for a case on Westlaw will likely be different from the number of headnotes for the same case on Lexis.

The text of each headnote often comes directly from the text of the opinion. But because only the opinion itself is authoritative, do not rely only on headnotes in doing research and do not cite them in legal documents. At the beginning of each headnote is a number identifying it in sequence with other headnotes; this means the headnotes act somewhat like a table of contents. Within the text of the opinion, the same sequence number will appear in bold font or be enclosed in brackets at the point in the text supporting the headnote. Online, the sequence number may link directly from the headnote to the relevant portion of the text. Read and cite that text, not the headnote. Just after the sequence number, each headnote begins with a word or phrase in bold print. These are used in subject indexes to locate other cases that discuss similar points of law. For example, the Figure 9.2 is an image from Lexis for *State v. Hart* shows the first headnote is about Criminal Law and Procedure.

Figure 9.2. Lexis Headnote from *State v. Hart*

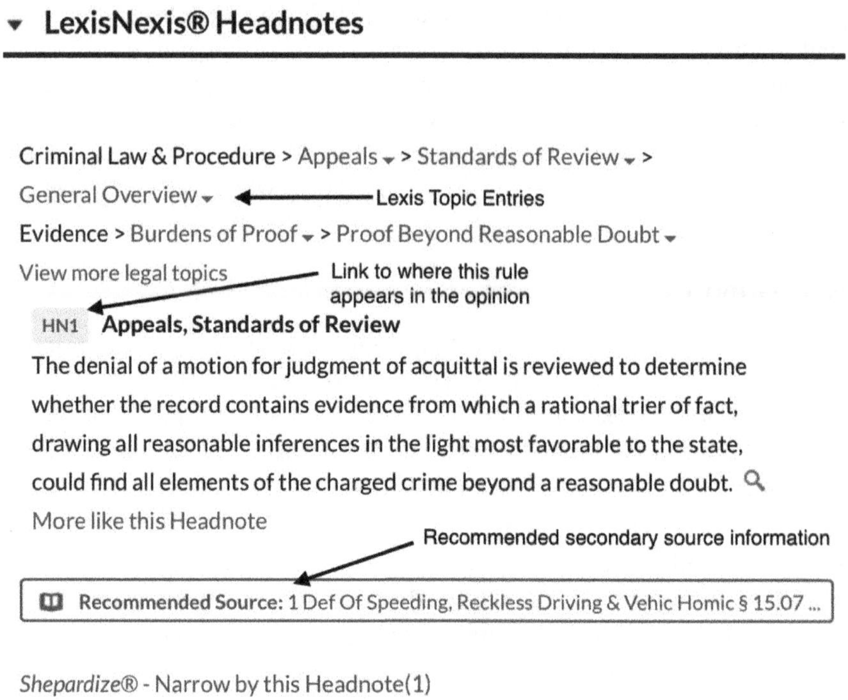

Reprinted with permission from LexisNexis

Figure 9.3. Westlaw Headnote from *State v. Hart*

Reprinted from Westlaw with permission from Thomson Reuters

On Westlaw, the phrases to the right of the key icon provide two specific criminal law topics that the headnote addresses. Clicking on Criminal Law or on one of the subtopics would take you to a database where Westlaw has compiled other headnotes on the same topics (see Figure 9.3).

You can use headnotes as research tools in the following ways, as explained in the Research Strategies part of this chapter:

- Use the headnote reference as a searchable term,
- Click on a relevant headnote in a case you have already found, and
- Look in a database containing headnotes.

G. Library References

Some reporters give cross references to the relevant sections of a legal encyclopedia like *Corpus Juris Secundum* (CJS). A summary of the law in a legal encyclopedia could provide valuable background information and refer to additional cases or statutes that are on point.

H. Procedural information

Reporters contain a variety of procedural information on each case, including the court from which the case was appealed, the name of the trial court judge, the appellate judges who heard the case, and the judge who wrote the appellate decision. Note that following a judge's name may be "C.J." for the chief judge, "P.J." for the presiding judge in the Court of Appeals, or "J." for another judge.

When a case is decided *per curiam*, no judge is given credit as author of the court's opinion. If a case includes concurring or dissenting opinions, they will be noted in the procedural listings. Also in this section will be the attorneys who argued for each party.

I. Disposition

The disposition of the case is the court's decision to affirm, reverse, remand, or vacate the decision below. If the appellate court agrees with only part of the lower court's decision, the appellate court may affirm in part and reverse in part.

J. Opinion

The actual opinion of the court begins with the name of the judge who wrote the opinion, given in bold. If the appellate judges who heard the case do not agree on the outcome or the reasons for the outcome, they may write separate opinions. An appellate case may have one opinion or several.

- The *majority opinion* is supported by a majority of the judges and determines the outcome of the case.
- A *concurring opinion* is written by a judge who agrees with the outcome but not the reasoning of the majority.
- A *dissenting opinion* is written by a judge who disagrees with the outcome supported by the majority of the judges.

While only the majority opinion is binding precedent, the other opinions provide valuable insights and may be cited as persuasive authority. If no opinion has the support of more than half of the judges, the case will be decided by whichever opinion garners the most support. The result is a *plurality decision.*

V. Research Strategies for Finding Cases

Lawyers typically find references to relevant cases throughout the research process. For example, you might find case citations in a secondary source (see Chapter 3) or by using an annotated statute (see Chapter 5). Also, a supervisor or colleague might have provided one good case, which you used to find other cases by looking at the cases cited in the opinion, or by using a citator such as Shepard's or KeyCite. However, just because you have found cases using a few methods, you should still use all the strategies available to ensure that your research is thorough (see Table 9.5). This section will discuss all the research strategies that were introduced in Chapter 2, in the context of researching cases.

Table 9.5. Search Strategies Checklist for Cases

- Find by citation
- Search by topic
- Search with natural language
- Search with Boolean language
- Set search parameters
- Use filters
- Use citators

A. Find by Citation

Many secondary sources provide citations or links to relevant cases, and some secondary sources analyze cases in depth (see Chapter 3). If your issue is governed by statute, you might find citations to relevant cases by using the annotations to the statutes (see Chapter 5). Also, you might have one good case that you can use to find other cases by looking at the cases that are cited in the one good case. Type the citation into the search bar of a website or platform (i.e. Google Scholar, Lexis, Westlaw).

B. Search by Topic

Lexis and Westlaw have created case finding tools based on topics and subtopics to make research easier.

1. Topic System on Lexis

Table 9.6. Methods of Using the Topic System

- Use a link to Topics on the Lexis home page then search or browse.
- Use the topic links in a relevant headnote from a case you know is on point.

Lexis indexes cases using a Topic system. Lexis has designated 44 topics. Each topic is divided into subtopics. For example, under the topic Real Property Law, there is a subtopic of Adverse Possession. Adverse Possession is then divided into the topics Adverse Possession Procedure, Defenses, Elements of Adverse Claims, General Overview, and Government Entity Claims. If you select one of those topics, you will get a list of cases categorized under that topic. You can then use filters on the left side to narrow your results. For example, you can use the "Court" filter to narrow to a specific jurisdiction. Lexis indexes each headnote of each case according to these Topics and subtopics. Table 9.6 summarizes the methods for using this Topic system.

a. Topics Link on Lexis Home Page

From the Lexis home page, use the "Explore" menu to find the Topics tab. You can then enter search terms in the "Search Topics" box, or browse the topics listed. For example, if you are researching the adverse possession issue, you could enter "adverse possession" in the search box and then explore the topics and subtopics in the results. Also, you can browse the list of topics to find one that looks relevant, such as Real Property Law. If you click on the Real Property Law link, you will see a list of subtopics that can be expanded. Click on the plus sign to expand Adverse Possession and then explore the specific topics listed. For example, if you select "Elements of Adverse Claims," you will get a list of cases. If the list of cases is numerous, you can use the filters on the left side, such as the "Court" filter to narrow results to a specific jurisdiction.

b. Topic Link in a Case Headnote

Headnotes are useful tools for thorough case law research. If you have found a case that seems relevant, you can skim the headnotes of that case to find particular points of law that are important for your issue. Above the headnote, Lexis lists the relevant topic and subtopics. If you select the down arrow next to the subtopic, you will see options for "Get Documents" and "Create Alert." If you select "Get Documents," you will get a list of cases which you can then filter using the options on the left side of the screen.

2. Topic and Key Number System on Westlaw

Table 9.7. Methods of Using the Topic and Key Number System

- Use a link to the Topic and Key Number System on the Westlaw home page.
- Use the key number linked in a relevant headnote from a case you know is on point.
- Use a Topic and Key Number as a search term in a search query.

One of the most effective ways to search Westlaw is with Key Numbers, available under "Content types" on the home page of Westlaw. The Topic and Key Number system indexes cases from all American jurisdictions according to more than 400 "Topics." Each Topic is an area of law, and Topics range from "Abandoned and Lost Property" to "Zoning and Planning."

West assigns a number to each of its 400+ Topics, placing them in alphabetical order. Adverse Possession, for example, has been assigned number 20. Within each Topic, the area of law is broken down into discrete subtopics. These subtopics are called "Key Numbers," and each begins with the letter "k." Key Numbers can be represented by descriptive words (e.g., Exclusion of Others, Necessity) or the number assigned by West (e.g., 36, 58). An example of a Topic and Key Number for Adverse Possession cases dealing with exclusion of others from the property is 20k36. Often there are additional, even more discrete outline numbers in the Topics and Key Numbers on Westlaw. For example, the Topic and Key Number for Adverse Possession 16, "Acts of Ownership in General," has three subheadings: (1) In general; (2) Marking boundaries and entry to make survey; and (3) Wild lands.

West indexes each headnote of each case reported in West's National Reporter System according to these Topics and Key Numbers. The headnotes that appear in the Key Number digest are the same headnotes that appear at the beginning of West cases. Some researchers find it helpful to analogize the Key Number digest of indexing cases online to hashtags on Instagram.[6] Table 9.7 summarizes methods for using the Key Number system.

a. Topic and Key Number Link on Westlaw Home Page

First, you can simply go to the "Topics & Key Numbers" link under "Content types" and open a directory of all 400+ Topics. Browse the directory and select those Topics that seem most relevant to your work. Open a Topic by clicking on it and selecting the relevant Key Number (or the range of Key Numbers).

As an example, to find cases about the necessity of proving hostile possession in an adverse possession claim, and what that element requires, go to West's list of Topics and select "Adverse Possession." Then click on the portion of the outline labeled "Hostile Character of Possession"; it appears in Part I, Section F. Clicking on "58 Necessity" will lead to a list of the headnotes of all cases that West has indexed under that one Topic and Key Number. Scrolling through the results will lead to the headnotes. Note that a case will be listed in the digest for each of its headnotes that are indexed under that Topic and Key Number; thus, a case may appear more than once. Another option is to use the search bar at the top of the Topics directory. The search will review West headnotes for your search terms. Filters are available on the left side of the screen.

b. Key Number from a Relevant Case

A second approach to using the Key Number System is to start with a Topic and Key Number from a relevant case. Once you have a case that is relevant to your work, review its headnotes. When you find a headnote that is on point, clicking on the Topic or on one level of the Key Number will lead to the list of cases indexed by the Key Number System under the related Topic and Key Number.

c. Topic and Key Number as a Search Term

A third way to use the Topics and Key Numbers from West's Key Number System is to conduct a search with a relevant Topic and Key Number as the search term. For best results, use this option only as an advanced search,

---

6. You might hear some practitioners or professors refer to the "creating a digest" or "using a digest" of cases. What they mean is using the Topic and Key Number System to gather a collection of cases on a particular topic/subtopic. "Digest" is a term that refers back to the print volumes that listed cases under the Topics and Key Numbers.

either entering "adv:" before the Topics and Key Numbers or clicking on "Advanced" to the right of the search bar. For example, the search *adv: 20k58* produces a highly relevant, small set of cases about hostile possession in an adverse possession claim. You can also add other terms to the search. To use this method effectively, you should keep a running list of relevant Topics and Key Numbers. This allows you to use Topics and Key Numbers throughout the research process and can be useful for future research projects if you have a repeat issue.

Regardless of how you access and use the Key Number System, remember that the Topics and Key Numbers are the same in all American jurisdictions. If you needed to find California cases on adverse possession, simply follow the steps outlined above, but change the jurisdiction to California. The resulting Topics and Key Numbers will be the same, but the cases indexed will be from California.

C. Search Full Text with Natural Language and Boolean Language (Terms and Connectors)

Table 9.8. Steps for Searching with Natural and Boolean Language

- Set search parameters (narrow the database so you get the most relevant results)
- Start with broad terms in a natural language search
- Filter results if you get many cases
- Skim results to learn new search terms
- Think about synonyms, exact phrases, proximity of words
- Focus on the legal issue (not specific facts) to come up with search terms
- Construct a Boolean search (see Chapter 2 for in-depth discussion of Boolean Language)
- Use filters after you run a search

Full-text searching is a popular and effective way to retrieve cases that will allow you analyze your research question. Table 9.8 shows the steps for using language searching.

1. Creating Searches

Regardless of the service you are using for full-text searching, creating effective searches can yield the most useful cases. Chapter 2 of this book explains both natural language searching and Boolean searching and outlines common connectors and commands for Boolean searching. Take a moment before you begin throwing words in a search bar to consider the key terms that are likely to appear in relevant documents.

These two tips can help you create effective searches: First, searches should be broad enough to be comprehensive but specific enough to avoid getting results that will not be helpful. If you are looking for cases about discrimination in housing, you likely don't need to read cases about discrimination in transportation, employment, or other areas. Second, if you can identify the legal issue, try developing searches based on the issue rather than on the specific facts of your client's situation. Fact-intensive searches can be too narrow, returning no results (e.g., you searched for "boot" instead of "shoe"); they can also return results that are legally irrelevant (e.g., a contract for delivery of boots or a defendant charged with using a boot as a dangerous weapon).

2. Natural Language

If you are unsure what documents or issues you are looking for, start with broad terms, perhaps in a natural language search. Sometimes, you can get a good start by entering a few thoughtful words in the search bar or entering the legal question that is presented in your problem. Natural language searching on Lexis and Westlaw tends to produce good results; however, you might get more results than you want to sift through, so you will want to use filters to limit your results.

3. Boolean Language

Even though natural language searching is quite sophisticated, to be thorough, you will want to create a list of potential searches using different search terms and connectors. In creating these searches, anticipate the types of documents that might be relevant to your issues and where key terms might appear in those documents. Would they be in the same sentence or the same paragraph? Are you looking for a specific term that is always presented the same way or do you need to look for alternative language? Creating Boolean searches after you have used other search strategies and read some cases is a good approach since you will have a better idea of the types of terms and phrases that are likely to be present in the court opinions.

D. Set Search Parameters

Many online providers allow you to restrict your search by jurisdiction and content. In other words, you should set parameters on your search so that you can view just Oregon cases. You might be able to limit further by excluding federal cases that originated in Oregon, or by selecting the cases of just one level of Oregon court: the Oregon Supreme Court, the Oregon Court of Appeals, or the Oregon Tax Court.

You can find these databases in several ways.

- In the universal search bar on Lexis or Westlaw, begin typing *Oregon cases* (or a more specific search for a particular court) and you may see a list of relevant databases. Click on the title of the database you wish to search.
- On the provider's home page, you might be able to select a particular state and content type (e.g., click on a link "State Materials" and then "Oregon," and review the databases listed under "Cases.") Whichever approach you take, always look for the small "i" or "?" icon next to the name of the database to learn its exact coverage.
- After you type a search query into the universal search bar, you might have the option to select "Oregon" as the jurisdiction.

E. Filter Results

After running a search, you might be able to filter the results to tailor them more narrowly. Especially if your initial search returns hundreds of cases, filtering can help you locate the most important. You might filter by jurisdiction, excluding cases from other states and focusing just on Oregon Supreme Court cases. You might filter out older cases. Another helpful filter is the reported status of the cases; those cases published in reporters carry more weight than *unpublished cases* that appear only in online resources. In addition, you can filter according to particular words that appear in the document. Filters often appear in the left margin of the screen.

Regardless of the restrictions and filters you apply, you may be able to sort the resulting list of cases. This sorting does not eliminate cases from the list (as filtering does) but arranges them in a particular order: by relevance (based on the service provider's algorithm), by date, by court, by how often the cases have been cited, and by the frequency of your search terms.

F. Use a Citator to Update Cases and Expand Research

As mentioned in Chapter 2, you will be updating continuously throughout your research to make sure your research is thorough and that the statute, case, or other primary source you are using is still valid and current. When you are engaged in updating, you are trying (1) to find other sources that impact the case you are updating, and (2) to find other sources that assist your analysis and expand your research universe. Table 9.9 gives you the checklist to use when updating a case.

Table 9.9. Checklist for Updating

- Access Citator Lists
- Analyze Citator Symbols and Tools
- Limit Citator Results

Below are two examples of updating a case using Shepard's on Lexis and Keycite on Westlaw.

1. Shepard's on Lexis

The following explanation uses *State v. Hart*, 222 Or App 285 (2008), to demonstrate updating with Shepard's on Lexis (see Figure 9.4).

Figure 9.4. Shepard's Report for *State v. Hart*

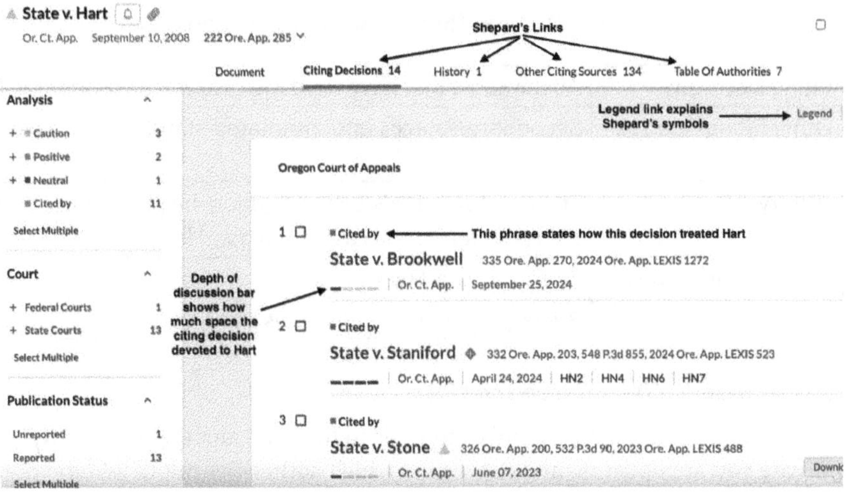

Reprinted with permission from LexisNexis

a. Access the Citator Lists

You can access Shepard's on Lexis in three ways:

- When viewing the document, click on one of the links at the top of the page. Alternatively, click on the "Shepardize document" link on the right of the screen.
- Click the Shepard's symbol that appears near the title of a document. For example, clicking the yellow triangle next to *State v. Hart* will open the Shepard's report for "Citing Decisions" for that case.
- Use the general search bar and type shep: followed by the citation (e.g., shep: 222 Or App 285).

These methods are summarized in Table 9.10.

Table 9.10. Links for Shepard's Information

Citing Decisions	All the cases that have cited the case you are updating.
Other Citing Sources	Secondary sources and annotated statutes that have cited your case.
History	The full story of this case's litigation, helping you decide whether the case is still good law.
Table of Authorities	The cases cited by your case.
Filings	Briefs, pleadings, and motions citing your case.

b. Analyze the Citator Symbols and Tools

Lexis uses a variety of symbols and tools to help you analyze the validity of the case you are updating and determine which authorities might add to your research (see Table 9.11 for a list of these symbols). You can sort the display of documents in the list of Citing Decisions using a menu to the right of the screen, called "Display Settings." The sorting choices are level of court (highest to lowest in the court system), discussion (how much space the case devotes to yours), analysis (negative, positive, or neutral treatment of your case), and date (from the newest case to the oldest). You can control the amount of information displayed in a list of Citing Decisions, again by using "Display Settings." To view a list of case names, along with their citations and brief excerpts, select "Full View." To see just the case names and citations of the Citing Decisions, click "Title View."

Table 9.11. Shepard's Color Codes and Other Symbols

Color Blocks	Shepard's color codes the analytical treatment descriptions, ranging from most negative (red) and cautionary (yellow) to positive (green), and neutral (blue). In the full view of Citing Decisions, a colored block precedes a few words explaining the way that case treated yours. For example, "distinguished by" is accompanied by a yellow block; "followed by" will have a green block.
Red Stop Sign	The case you are updating has negative treatment.
Orange Q	The case you are updating has its validity questioned by citing sources.
Yellow Triangle	The case you are updating has possible negative treatment.
Green Plus	The case you are updating has positive treatment.
Blue Octagon with an "I"	Citing information available.

The placement of these symbols matters greatly. A symbol next to the name of the case you are updating provides a summary of its validity. In the *Hart* example, a yellow triangle appears at the top left of the screen because two cases—*Lewis* and *Wright*—have distinguished *Hart*, noting that their facts are different from the facts in that case. In *Hart*, the victim received a gash in the head, while in *Lewis* the victim's hair was pulled and in *Wright* the victim was bruised.

These symbols also appear after the name of each citing decision, where they show how later cases have treated each of those citing decisions. That is confusing, so consider the *Hart* example. *Hart* has a yellow triangle because *Lewis* and *Wright* distinguish it. The *Lewis* case has itself received cautionary treatment, so it has a yellow triangle, too. However, the *Wright* case has been cited by just four cases, with little discussion, so its symbol is a neutral "I" in a blue octagon.

The cases listed in the Shepard's report will display the Shepard's symbol, citation of the case, date, a bar graph that shows depth of treatment, headnote numbers indicating the headnote topics addressed in the citing source, and an analytical phrase indicating how the citing source is treating your case.

c. Limit the Citator Results

Shepard's provides filters in the left frame for limiting the number of documents you review. If you don't see them, click "Filters" on the left side of the screen to display the following filters: Analysis, Court, Publication Status, Discussion, Headnotes, Timeline. Under "Narrow by" is a box where you can enter search terms. Each of these filters can be expanded or collapsed.

2. KeyCite on Westlaw

Updating a case on Westlaw using KeyCite is very similar to the process of updating on Lexis with Shepard's. The terms used are sometimes different and the type and location of various icons will vary, but the concepts are the same. The following discussion uses *State v. Hart*, 222 Or App 285 (2008), as an example of updating a case.

a. Access the Citator Lists

You can access KeyCite on Westlaw in three ways:

- Retrieve the document and click on one of the KeyCite links at the top of the Westlaw screen, just above the document's heading. Each case has several links: Filings, Negative Treatment, History, Citing References, and Table of Authorities.
- Click on a KeyCite status flag next to the name of the case, either in the document itself or in a list of search results. Note that this will take you to one of the citation lists, Negative Treatment. From there, you can select one of the other links as well.
- Type kc: or keycite: followed by the case citation in Westlaw's universal search box. Again, this approach will take you to Negative Treatment, where you can select another link, too.

Table 9.12 provides a list of links for KeyCite information.

Table 9.12. Links for KeyCite Information

Filings	Briefs and motions filed in litigation of the case. Read these documents to see additional arguments made and authorities supporting those arguments.
History	Opinions in the same litigation as your case (positive and negative). (Example—the opinion on a motion earlier in the litigation as well as a subsequent appellate decision). You can restrict the History list even further from the drop-down menu next to "View," by selecting from Principal History, Previous History, Subsequent History, or Negative Direct History.
Negative Treatment	Cases with negative impact on your case (negative history and additional cases that treated the decision negatively).
Citing References	All cases, administrative decisions, secondary sources, court filings from other litigation, and other documents that have cited the case you are updating. A drop-down menu to the right of the Citing References link shows the number of documents in each category (e.g., cases, secondary sources) and allows you to open to just that subset of documents.
Table of Authorities	The cases cited by your case.

b. Analyze Citator Symbols

Westlaw uses a variety of symbols and tools to help you analyze the validity of the case you are updating and determine which authorities might add to your research (see Table 9.13). While similar in function to Lexis, Westlaw uses different symbols. You can sort the documents in citing references by date, by depth of treatment, or by court. Use the drop-down menu under "Sort By." This tool does not filter out any of the items listed but arranges them according to your selection.

Table 9.13. KeyCite Flags and Other Symbols

Red Flag	West has determined the case is no longer good law for at least one legal point, perhaps because it was overruled or reversed. The case might still be binding authority for other points, so you must read and analyze each citing source yourself to determine its impact on a case you are updating or to decide whether to include it in your expanded research.
Yellow Flag	West has found some negative authority for the case, but it has not been overruled or reversed.
Blue and White Striped Flag	The case is on appeal to a federal circuit court or to the U.S. Supreme Court.
Orange Exclamation Mark	Warning that a case relies on an authority that has been overruled or is invalid, undermining the case.
Quotation Marks	The source quoted your case.

c. Interpret the Citing References

It is not enough to just look at the symbols. Westlaw provides analytical information to help you determine how your case has been affected by citing sources. Table 9.14 summarizes this analytical information.

Table 9.14. Types of Information for Each Citing Source

Treatment of the case	How the citing source treated your case (e.g., reversed, distinguished, discussed, examined, cited). This is the most important information for determining whether your case is still good law.
Flag for citing reference	To the right of the treatment column, you might see a flag, next to the name of the citing reference. That flag indicates how the citing reference was treated by later cases. It does not indicate how the citing reference treated your case.
Title and date of the case	Name of the document that cites your case and the date it was decided. Underneath the title is a citation to that document. If you choose "More detail" or "Most detail" from a drop-down menu, a brief excerpt where the document cited your case.
Type of document	When using citing references for sources other than cases, the description under the heading "Type" will indicate what type of document the source is.
Depth of treatment	The bars in the "Depth" column indicate how much each citing reference discusses your case. 4 bars = more than one page 3 bars = more than one paragraph 2 bars = less than one paragraph 1 bar = a brief mention (typically in a string citation)
Headnotes	The headnote topics covered by a citing source. As you point to each headnote number, the headnote text appears, making it easy to determine whether that point of law is relevant to your research.

d. Limit the Citator Results

You can limit the documents in the KeyCite list by using filters in the margin of the screen. You can narrow the list by document type (cases, secondary sources, court documents). Once you have selected a document type, you can narrow your list further by using specific terms in the "search within results" box and by using filters specific to the document type. For example, filters for cases include jurisdiction, date, depth of treatment, headnote topic, treatment status, and whether the citing reference is a reported or an unreported case. The "+" symbol in front of the filter expands choices for that filter. For example, expanding the filter for jurisdiction allows you to restrict results by the federal or state jurisdictions in which courts have cited your case.

VI. Selecting Cases to Read In-Depth

Each of these research strategies, from finding by citation to using a citator, will produce a list of potentially relevant cases. To decide which cases in the results list to read in-depth, consider the guidelines in Table 9.15.

Table 9.15. Guidelines for Selecting Cases to Read In-Depth

Jurisdiction	If you are working on an Oregon issue, cases from Oregon will almost always be more important than cases decided elsewhere, which are just persuasive authority.
Treatment	Look for negative treatment, indicating that a later case has reversed, overruled, criticized, or distinguished your case.
Court	Begin reading cases from the Oregon Supreme Court, then the Oregon Court of Appeals. When trial court decisions are included, read those trial court decisions last.
Date	Start with more recent cases rather than older cases.
Headnotes	Select cases that were cited for the headnotes that are most relevant to your project.
Search Terms	Use keywords to narrow the citator results to those that contain an important fact or legal term.
Depth of Treatment	Cases that devote more space to your case (shown by depth of treatment bars) are likely to be more helpful than others that merely cite your case.

Never disregard a binding, factually similar case simply because that case reaches a result that would be bad for your client. You must either find a way to distinguish that case or find an alternative legal basis for your claim. Finally, in reading the citing sources, look for trends in how often each case is cited and what treatment it receives. You should generally base your analysis on cases that have been cited and followed frequently.

VII. Strategic Reading of Cases

As you begin reading cases, the following strategies, introduced in Chapter 1 and summarized in Table 9.16, may help you understand them more quickly and thoroughly.

Table 9.16. Strategic Reading Checklist

Before reading	• Determine and connect with your professional purpose • Articulate how the case connects to your pre-existing knowledge • Establish the context of the case: note the date of the case; consider the social and procedural context; note the identity of the parties • Create an organized plan for reading
During reading	• Read all the headings and other structural aspects of the case (i.e. the first sentence of each paragraph) before you read the case carefully • Comprehend the facts • Predict what you will learn from the case • Think about what questions will be answered • Develop new questions as you are reading • Create graphic depictions of ideas, topics, and subtopics • Annotate the case with your questions and observations • Paraphrase what you are reading • Look up terms and solve confusions before you move on in your reading • Identify the main ideas in the issue, holding, and court's reasoning • Identify the legal rules
After reading	• Evaluate the court's reasoning • Brief the case • Ask yourself questions • Ask questions to others (professors, colleagues) • Connect the case to your existing knowledge and experiences • Determine how the case fits with other cases and write a synthesis

A. Before Reading

Reading and comprehending judicial opinions requires deep concentration. Therefore, prepare your environment to facilitate that concentration. Some researchers prefer to print key cases, as reading them in hard copy enhances understanding. If you prefer to read cases online, close other windows on your computer to help avoid interruptions and distractions; use a larger screen so you see more context and understand the text better; and use the platform's features that allow you to highlight and annotate text, so you are reading actively.

Think about your role and why you are reading the case. What is your professional goal in reading the case? Read the synopsis, headnotes, or portions of the case to determine whether the case seems to be on point and to reflect on the context of the case. Think about your existing knowledge of the legal issue or topic involved so you can connect the case to that knowledge.

Create an organized plan for reading. Sort the cases according to jurisdiction and then by decision date. If the law at issue has several elements or factors, you might also organize the cases according to the elements or factors they discuss. Then, begin with the most recent case to find the current rule of law and read the rest in reverse chronological order. As an alternative, some researchers read cases chronologically to learn how the law developed over time. The key is to define your goal and organize the order in which you read the cases accordingly.

B. During Reading

In addition to the headnotes, read headings and the first sentence of each paragraph to understand the structure of the analysis. Then skim the entire case for an overview of what happened and why so you can comprehend the facts. Focus more attention on the most relevant parts of the case, indicated by a headnote or highlighted search terms. Next read the case slowly and interactively using some or all of the following strategies: predict what questions will be answered by the case; develop new questions while you are reading; create graphic depictions of ideas, topics, and subtopics; annotate the case with questions and observations; paraphrase or summarize each paragraph or section that you have just read; look up terms and solve confusions before moving on in your reading; identify and note the issues, holdings, rules and reasoning. The more interactive and didactic your reading is, the more you will understand the case, which will, in turn, make subsequent research more effective.

C. After Reading

After you have read the case thoroughly, you might read it again at the same time as you take notes or create a formal "case brief" where you include the important facts, identify the issue, summarize the holding, and explain the reasoning. The notes might instead be more informal notes that only you can understand. Regardless of the form, the process of taking notes will help you sort through, identify, and comprehend the essential concepts of the case. In law school, the notes will record your understanding of the case both for class discussion and for the end of the semester when you begin to review for exams. When preparing to write a legal document, the notes will assist you in organizing your analysis into an outline.

Pay attention to how cases fit together. Has the law in this jurisdiction remained unchanged or have new elements been introduced? Has the meaning of an important term been redefined? Have certain facts virtually guaranteed success for one party while other facts have tended to cause difficulties? Does one case summarize the current rule, or do you have to synthesize a rule from several cases that each address part of the rule? Creating a quick chart of cases — including the name, date, jurisdiction, elements, facts, and key ideas — can help here. Look for trends in the law and in the facts of the cases. Then carefully consider how the synthesized cases affect your research project.

Chapter 10

Researching Tribal Law

CHAPTER GOALS

After reading this chapter, you will be able to

1. Find information about the legal relationship between Tribes and Oregon;
2. Find basic information about tribal jurisdiction;
3. Identify sources of law pertaining to tribes;
4. Search for secondary tribal law sources; and
5. Search for primary tribal law sources.

I. Relationship between Tribal Law Research and Oregon Legal Research

Tribal law is the law Indian tribes enforce for their own members and territories. It is different from federal Indian law, which is the law concerning the relationship between federal, state, and tribal governments. It is also distinct from Oregon state law; however, because there are nine federally recognized tribes in the State of Oregon (185,723 indigenous living in the 36 Oregon counties),[1] you should be familiar with the basic sources involved with researching tribal law.

Tribal law is frequently overlooked in legal education even though it is an important part of the U.S. legal landscape. However, legal information professionals are highlighting the importance of teaching Indian and tribal law and calling for its inclusion in legal research and writing programs.

1. *Introduction to Native Peoples of Oregon*, Oregon Blue Book: Almanac and Fact Book, https://sos.oregon.gov/blue-book/Pages/national-tribes-intro.aspx.

> Graduates with an awareness of tribal law will be better equipped to serve tribal communities, recognize and research tribal law issues when they arise, and contribute to the broader legal discourse surrounding Native American rights and interests.... This knowledge does not just benefit those working directly with or for Tribal Nations; it is essential for all legal professionals given that tribes interact extensively with federal and state governments, businesses, and individuals. Understanding tribal law empowers legal professionals to effectively address legal issues in Indian Country and contribute to a more inclusive legal system.[2]

Tribal governments are separate sovereigns with the power to protect the health, safety, and welfare of their members, as well as govern their lands. Oregon has a government-to-government relationship with tribal governments as directed in *Oregon Revised Statutes* §§ 182.162 to 182.168.

II. Finding Information on Tribes and Tribal Government

A. Research Guides

A helpful first step to researching tribal law, is to consult a research guide, which will provide advice on process, as well as identify helpful secondary and primary sources. To find a research guide, type search terms such as *tribal law research guide* into a search engine search bar. Table 10.1 provides examples of these.

2. Madole, Amber and Shucha, Bonnie J. & Plevel, Rebecca, Integrating Tribal Law into the Legal Research & Writing Curriculum: Benefits, Challenges, and Strategies (May 28, 2024). Univ. of Wisconsin Legal Studies Research Paper No. 1806, 31 Perspectives 4 (2024), Available at SSRN: https://ssrn.com/abstract=4845919.

Table 10.1. Examples of Research Guides

- "Researching American Indian Tribal Law" by David E. Selden is a short article published in *The Colorado Lawyer* in 2014 and provides basic tips for research, http://www.narf.org/nill/documents/selden_article_tribal_law.pdf.
- The National Indian Law Library's website also links to Indian Law Research Guides, http://www.narf.org/nill/resources/index.html.
- Indigenous Peoples Law and Policy Resource Guide: American Indian Law, https://law-arizona.libguides.com/lawlibrary/IPLP_resource_guide_american_indian_law.
- Indian and Tribal Law Research Guide, University of Oregon, https://researchguides.uoregon.edu/Indian-TribalLaw.
- Native American Law Research Guide, Georgetown Law Library, https://guides.ll.georgetown.edu/nativeamericanlaw.

B. Tribal Websites

Tribal websites have an abundance of information, from government information to newsletters, to tribal history. See Table 10.2 for a list of tribes in Oregon and their websites.

Table 10.2. Tribes in Oregon

Burns Piute Tribe	https://burnspaiute-nsn.gov
Confederated Tribes of Coos, Lower Umpqua and Siuslaw Indians	https://ctclusi.org
Confederated Tribes of Grand Ronde	https://www.grandronde.org
Confederated Tribes of Siletz Indians	https://ctsi.nsn.us
Confederated Tribes of the Umatilla Indian Reservation	https://ctuir.org
Confederated Tribes of Warm Springs	https://warmsprings-nsn.gov
Cow Creek Band of Umpqua Tribe of Indians	https://www.cowcreek-nsn.gov
Coquille Indian Tribe	https://www.coquilletribe.org
Klamath Tribes	https://klamathtribes.org

C. Government Websites

For general information on tribes and tribal law in Oregon, you can consult the Legislative Commission on Indian Services[3] and the Oregon Blue Book.[4]

III. Sources of Law Pertaining to Tribes

The research process for tribal law is similar to the process introduced in Chapter 1. Starting with secondary sources may be helpful. Then, you may want to gather information about the tribe and the types of primary sources you will need for your research. The National Indian Law Library's Tribal Law Gateway,[5] is an index of tribes, listing sources for tribal constitutions, codes, and judicial opinions. The National Indian Law Library also provides helpful "How to Find" tips for locating the sources you may need.

The Oregon Legislative Commission on Indian Services (OLCIS),[6] as well as the Oregon Blue Book,[7] provide information on the nationally recognized tribes in Oregon as well as other information. Both the OLCIS and Oregon Blue Book websites provide links to the tribes' websites. Tribe websites may provide links to tribal codes and other documents, as well as other governmental information.

A. Secondary Sources for Tribal Law

1. Overview

Secondary sources such as treatises and articles provide general information about tribal jurisdiction and tribal governments, as well as specific topical information, such as Indian gaming, child welfare, climate change, and water rights. Table 10.3 provides examples of secondary sources related to tribal law.

3. https://www.oregonlegislature.gov/cis.
4. https://sos.oregon.gov/blue-book/Pages/national-tribes-intro.aspx.
5. http://www.narf.org/nill/triballaw/index.html.
6. https://www.oregonlegislature.gov/cis#.
7. https://sos.oregon.gov/blue-book/Pages/national-tribes.aspx.

Table 10.3. Examples of Secondary Sources

American Indian Tribal Law, Mathew L. M. Fletcher
American Indian Tribal Governments, Sharon O'Brien
Introduction to Tribal Legal Studies, Justin B. Richland and Sarah Deer.
Fostering State-Tribal Collaboration, Andrea Wilkins
Tribal Constitutionalism: States, Tribes, and the Governance of Membership, Kirsty Gover
American Indian Law Journal
NARF Legal Review
Tribal Law Journal

2. Research Strategies for Finding Secondary Sources

To find secondary sources for tribal law, you will use the same basic research strategies discussed in Chapter 2 (Research Strategies) and Chapter 3 (Secondary Sources). In addition to using an academic library catalog, Lexis, and Westlaw, you will be looking at some additional websites and databases that specialize in tribal law information. This part of the chapter will discuss different methods of finding various secondary sources on tribal law.

a. Library Catalog

Academic law library catalogs are good places to search for both print and online resources. Use search terms that identify the topic you are interested in, and then filter by date, subject, author, or resource type, to refine your results. You can do similar searches on the State of Oregon Law Library website and the Law Library of Congress.

b. National Indian Law Library

The National Indian Law Library, Tribal Law Gateway, refers to several sources that will help you with the research process. For example, for help researching treaties, you can read Indian Treaties: A Bibliography published in the Law Library Journal[8] as well as consult several online tools such as the *IDA Treaties Explorer* from the Indigenous Digital Archive or *Indian Affairs: Laws*

8. Beth DeFelice, *Indian Treaties: A Bibliography*, 107:2 Law Lib. J. 241 (2015).

and Treaties from Oklahoma State University. You can also fine a collection of research guides, as well as Indian Law Bulletins, a current awareness service.

c. Institutional Repositories

The University of Oklahoma Law School publishes the *American Indian Law Review*, which you can access through their law school website. The University of New Mexico Law School publishes the *Tribal Law Journal*. The *Tribal Law Journal* web page provides access to current and past issues of the journal, as well as other resources.

d. Lexis and Westlaw

1. Using Search Parameters

On Lexis, under the Practice Area tab, select Native American Law to access primary and secondary sources. Secondary sources *include American Indian Law Review*, *Native American Law Emerging Issues*, *Restatement of Law: The Law of American Indians*, and *Tribal Law Journal*.

On Westlaw, select the Practice Areas tab and go to Native American Law. You will find a link to secondary sources, as well as other content types. Selecting secondary sources will lead you to a list of sources including *American Indian Law Deskbook*, *American Indian Law Review*, *Environmental Law in Indian Country*, and *Restatement of the Law: The Law of American Indians*.

2. Using Natural Language or Boolean Searching and Filters

Another research strategy on Lexis or Westlaw is to enter a search in the search bar and then use filters to narrow your results by practice Area or topic, or by source. For example, you could enter the search *tribal or Indian law and water rights* and then narrow your results by choosing a source filter such as American Indian Law Review.

e. Current Awareness Resources

Blogs and news sources are good avenues for tracking on tribal law. For example, National Indian Law Library News Blog covers current events in federal and tribal American Indian law. The blog archives reach back to 2007. Another excellent blog is Turtle Talk, a blog covering legal issues in Indian Country.

News sources focused on indigenous peoples and tribes include *First Nations Drum Newspaper*, *Indian Country Today*, Indianz.com, *Native American Times*, *Native News Online*, *National Native News*, *Native America Calling*, *Native America Today*, and the *Tribal College Journal*.

B. Primary Sources for Tribal Law

Table 10.4. Online Resources for Tribal Law

Native American Constitutions and Law Digitization Project	Tribal constitutions, codes and other legal documents
Tribal Court Clearinghouse	Tribal, state, and federal resources, Indian country subject-matter resources
Tribal Governments USA.gov	List of federally recognized tribes and resources for Native Americans
National Indian Law Library—Tribal Law Gateway	Information on tribes and resources on how to find codes, constitutions, court opinions, court rules, treaties and legal histories
Northwest Intertribal Court System	Consortium of tribes in the Northwest region of the U.S., with access to tribal court decisions
Law Library of Congress Indigenous Law Portal	American Indian constitutions and legal materials, research guides, and organization and agency information
Statewide Tribal Legislation Database	Information on state bills that affect tribal communities
Oregon Legislative Commission on Indian Services	Information on Oregon tribes
HeinOnline, Indigenous Peoples of the Americas: History, Culture, and Law	Subscription collection of primary and secondary legal sources in the areas of Indian and Tribal Law

1. Treaties

According to the National Museum of the American Indian, "treaties—solemn agreements between sovereign nations—lie at the heart of the relationship between Indian Nations and the United States."[9] Although not really considered tribal law, they establish geographic boundaries and prescribe con-

9. Smithsonian National Museum of the American Indian, *Nation to Nation: Treaties between the United States and American Indian Nations*, https://americanindian.si.edu/nationtonation/.

duct between the United States government and tribes. Therefore, finding treaties and other supporting documents will help provide historical context to the issues you are researching.

For an overview of the treaty process and a description of sources for researching treaties, read *Indian Treaties: A Bibliography.*[10] The official compilation of the public laws of the United States government, the *United States Statutes at Large*, contains the texts of Indian treaties. You can access the Statutes at Large multiple places online including the Government Printing Office website (Govinfo.gov), the Library of Congress, and HeinOnline.

Indian Affairs: Laws and Treaties[11] (often referred to as Kappler's) compiles U.S. treaties, laws, and executive orders relating to Indian tribes into a multi-volume set. It is available through Oklahoma State University digital library as well as HeinOnline.

There are other online resources that are helpful for researching treaties. The Indigenous Digital Archive Treaties Explorer[12] was created by the Museum of Indian Arts and Culture in partnership with the U.S. National Archives Office of Innovation and National Archives Foundation. This resource provides access to treaties, land cessions, and information on Native Nations. It also provides an interactive map where you can use your location, or enter a zip code or state name, to find documents related to treaties in your area.

The U.S. Congressional Serial Set contains U.S. House and Senate documents and reports, which can provide background information on treaty provisions between Indian tribes and the government. You can find the Serial Set on HeinOnline and Proquest Congressional. *American Indian and Alaska Native Documents in the Congressional Serial Set 1817–1899* is a database available through the University of Oklahoma College of Law Digital Commons. It compiles documents obtained from the serial set. The database allows you to search by type of document or year. It also has an interactive map that shows documents by specific geographic place.

Finally, the HeinOnline collection, Indigenous Peoples of the Americas: History, Culture, and Law, provides access to treaties and other treaty-related publications, as well as numerous other U.S. Government and tribal law resources.

10. Beth DiFelice, *Indian Treaties: A Bibliography*, 107 Law Libr. J. 241 (2015), Available at SSRN: https://ssrn.com/abstract=2669687.

11. Government Printing Office, *Indian Affairs: Laws and Treaties*, Charles J. Kappler ed. (1904).

12. https://digitreaties.org.

2. Enacted Law: Tribal Constitutions and Codes

For guidance on researching tribal constitutions and codes, consult the National Indian Law Library (NILL) Tribal Law Gateway.[13] This resource provides research strategies and refers to various free and subscription online resources, as well as print resources. You can search the NILL Collection of tribal constitutions and codes by using a search box provided on the page.

Other free sources of tribal constitutions and codes are the Indigenous Law Portal from the Library of Congress, the Indigenous Law Web Archive from the Library of Congress, the Tribal Court Clearinghouse, the Statewide Tribal Legislation Database from the National Conference of State Legislatures, the Native American Constitution and Law Digitization Project, and individual tribe websites. For example, if you go to the website for the Confederated Tribes of Siletz Indians and select the Government link, you will be able to access tribal ordinances, as well as tribal court information.

You can also access tribal constitutions and codes on subscription platforms such as Lexis, Westlaw, and HeinOnline. On Lexis, choose the Practice Area tab then link to the Native American Law database. You will find options to search all tribal codes or individual tribal codes. If you link to individual tribal codes and select a tribe, you will find codes, constitutions, court rules, and sometimes bylaws. Coverage varies by tribe.

Similarly, on Westlaw, select the Practice Area tab then click on the Native American Law link. You will find a link for Statutes and Court Rules — Tribal Codes that will lead you to a non-exhaustive list of tribes. You can use those links to find constitutions and codes.

HeinOnline's Indigenous Peoples of the Americas: History, Culture, and Law collection provides access to tribal codes, which you can browse by tribe. As far as tribes located in Oregon, only the Umatilla and Warm Springs tribal codes are included in the HeinOnline collection. Hein's collection also includes a "Constitutions, Acts & By-Laws" database that you can search with search terms or browse alphabetically. Table 10.4 lists sources for tribal law.

13. https://www.narf.org/nill/triballaw/codes.html.

3. Case Law

a. Free Resources

A good, free place to start is the National Indian Law Library, Tribal Court Gateway, "Find Tribal Courts and Court Opinions."[14] Also, the University of Washington Gallagher Law Library offers a helpful video on researching tribal court opinions in its Indian and Tribal Law Research Guide.

Researching tribal court opinions is very different from the case law research you have done for other jurisdictions. No single comprehensive resource (free or commercial) exists for researching tribal case law. If you are looking for tribal law material for one tribe, go the Tribal Law Gateway. For the particular tribe, the Tribal Law Gateway will list where to find tribal codes and constitutions, as well as court opinions. The resources will vary by tribe. Keep in mind that the Tribal Law Gateway refers to "Casemaker" which is an out-of-date reference. Casemaker merged with Fastcase, so those resources are now available on Fastcase.

National Indian Law Library, Indian Law Bulletins database,[15] is a current awareness service. According to the website, the Tribal Courts Bulletin highlights important cases decided by tribal courts that typically cite tribal law or include issues of jurisdiction, expulsion, disenrollment, tribal elections, judges, and civil matters between two tribal members. The Bulletin database contains the current bulleting as well as archives.

The Tribal Court Clearinghouse lists links to available tribal court decisions by the state where they are located. Under Oregon, you will find the Burns Paiute Tribal Court of Appeals cases, through the Northwest Intertribal Court System (NICS); the Confederated Tribes of Grand Ronde published opinions, through the tribe's website; Coquille Indian Tribal Court Opinions, through the tribe's website; and the Klamath Supreme Court decisions, through NICS.

Northwest Intertribal Court System is a consortium of tribes (Burns Paiute, Chehalis, Coleville, Hoh, Hoopa Valley, Jamestown S'Kallam, Kalispel, Klamath, Lummi, Muckleshoot, Nisqually, Port Gamble S'Kallam, Quileute, Samish, Sauk-Suiattle, Shoalwater Bay, Snoqualmie, Southern Ute, Squaxin Island, Stillaguamish, Tulalip, Upper Skagit, and Ute) and includes tribal court decisions from the late 1980s.[16]

---

14. https://www.narf.org/nill/triballaw/court.html.

15. https://www.narf.org/nill/bulletins/index.html.

16. Membership in the consortium changes occasionally. Check the website for current information. https://www.nics.ws/about.html.

The Caselaw Access Project from Harvard Law School provides PDF files of tribal court cases through West's American Tribal Law Reporter (1997–2017) with West's proprietary information removed.

b. Commercial Resources

As mentioned in Chapter 9, Fastcase is available through academic law libraries, as well as through the State of Oregon Law Library, and it is free for Oregon State Bar members. Choose jurisdiction, then select the down arrow by the "cases" box to see a list of tribal court opinions available. Select the box next to the tribe to include in your search. Select the "Save and Continue" button in the upper right corner, then enter you search terms in the search box.

HeinOnline's Indigenous Peoples of the Americas: History, Culture, and Law collection contains the Indian Law Reporter. The Indian Law Reporter (ILR) includes state and federal cases, in addition to tribal cases (the ILR did not include tribal cases until Volume 10). The National Indian Law Library has created an index[17] of only tribal court opinions for all volumes of the ILR. You can search this index with terms or browse by subject area.

On Lexis, under the Practice Area tab, select Native American Law, where you will find a database of tribal cases. You can choose to search "all tribal case" or search tribal cases by individual tribal court. In "Tribal Cases by Court," you can link to individual tribes and then search by several different fields or by terms. If you click the "i" icon next to the tribe's name, you will see information about coverage. For example, for the Burns Paiute Tribal Court of Appeals, the earliest decision is dated May 4, 1992, and the database has an "atypical" update schedule.

Westlaw has a database of tribal law cases in the Native American Law Practice Area. However, academic law library subscriptions do not include access to the full text of these cases. If you enter a search on Westlaw in the tribal cases database, you will see a case name and citation as well as an excerpt of the case; however, if you try to link to the case through an academic subscription, you will get a message that you do not have access. You can make a note of the citation, however, and go to the CaseLaw Access Project website (see above) and use the volume and page number to search for a PDF of the opinion.

---

17. https://www.narf.org/nill/ilr/.

Chapter 11

Research Process Examples

CHAPTER GOALS

After reading this chapter, you will be able to

1. Practice research process steps using free resources, Lexis, and Westlaw.
2. See examples of research strategies used in the context of free resources and commercial platforms.

I. Introduction

This book approaches legal research as a flexible but thoughtful process. The steps of that process are laid out in Chapter 1, Section I, and the chapters of this book have explained details of how to search for authorities (e.g., secondary sources, statutes, cases) using a variety of resources and search strategies. This chapter pulls all that information together to illustrate how to research an issue of Oregon state law in a legal area you have not researched previously. The illustrations here are generic so that they can be easily transferred to different projects. This chapter outlines three possible approaches.

The first example uses free sources, including Fastcase, which is freely available to Oregon Bar members; even if you have access to Lexis or Westlaw in practice, you will need to know how to use freely available or low-cost resources to conduct cost-effective research. The second uses Lexis to demonstrate generative AI strategies as well as term searching. The third uses Westlaw to demonstrate Boolean language searching. In practice, you could use a variety of sources in researching a single project, moving from Oregon BarBooks to Westlaw's Key Number System, to Shepard's on Lexis. The following approaches are intended to be illustrative, not limiting. An approach described for one source is probably available for others. In other words, the approach described below for Westlaw — using Boolean searches in selected databases — will also work on Lexis. Moreover, each of the three approaches shows just one of many possible routes a good researcher might follow on each platform and for each source. The beginning of each example starts with a table listing the relevant research strategies.

II. Researching with Free Resources

Table 11.1. Relevant Research Strategies Using Free Resources

Brainstorm with generative AI tools
Set search parameters
Browse a table of contents
Search an index
Search with a citation
Use statutory annotations
Search using natural language
Expand research with a citator

A. Conducting Pre-Research Tasks

Many of the sources you will search in this approach are restricted to Oregon. Consult with a law reference librarian to ensure that you know which Oregon resources are available and how to use them. If you are unsure of what is involved with your problem, or you need to generate ideas on issues statements or search terms, consider using a generative AI platform such as Claude AI to help with your brainstorming. After you complete some brainstorming, try to write your issue in one short, clear sentence.

B. Researching Secondary Sources

Begin with a natural language search on Google, using your issue statement as the search query. Skim the first twenty results quickly to see whether any seem helpful and reliable. If so, read them and record any references to primary sources (which you will need to confirm later as both accurate and current). If your Google search results are numerous and not very helpful, consider using a Google Advanced search and setting your search parameters to search for only *.gov* and *.org* domains. Create a Word document with a list of helpful

Google results, including each source's URL and a short note about why it is helpful. Your goal at this point is simply to get oriented.

Go to the Oregon BarBooks website. Members of the Oregon bar can link through the bar's website, while law school students might link through a law library's subscription. Once you log into your account, you will see a list of titles. Browse the list of titles for a few that seem to cover your issue. Open the link for each of those books, read the short description of its coverage, and browse the table of contents. Once you find a relevant book (or two), either download it and review its table of contents or search the index for relevant portions. Alternatively, you can use the BarBooks search bars to search for terms in a document title or in the document text to find a book. Once you select a title, you can search within that book using the search link at the top left of the screen. Early on in your research, you should read the first chapter of a relevant BarBook to get a clear overview of this area of law.

If the relevant area of law is covered by an Oregon-specific treatise, spend some time researching the treatise relevant to your issue. Free sources of treatises (print and online) include academic law libraries and large public law libraries. Try to select a treatise by an author with demonstrated expertise in a particular field, if possible. If you have not found anything helpful in the BarBooks or an Oregon treatise, turn to a general secondary source. Some public and academic law libraries still have print versions of American Jurisprudence, Corpus Juris Secundum, and American Law Reports.

C. Researching Oregon's Constitution, Statutes, and Regulations

If a constitutional provision is on point, you should have encountered it in researching secondary sources. Use the Oregon State Legislature's website to review the text of that provision and to find annotations to cases that discuss it. To be thorough, search the ORS index, which could refer you to additional provisions of the constitution.

You might have encountered an Oregon statute while researching secondary sources. If so, begin your statutory research by using the citation to find the statute. Be sure to read the current statute if you are giving advice prospectively, or to read the version of the statute in force when a past situation arose. Using the Oregon State Legislature's website, select the "Bills and Laws" tab, click on the relevant edition of the ORS, and enter the statute's citation in the appropriate box. As alternatives, you could use the "Search ORS" search bar in the center of the screen. Read the statute's language carefully. Then read any cross-referenced statutes, as well as statutes appearing just before or after the statute. Find and browse the table of contents for this portion of ORS and skim it, both to get an overview of the area of law and to see whether other statutes are on point. Even if you started this step with a citation to a particular statute, spend a few minutes searching the ORS General Index (located on the right side of the screen) to ensure that you haven't missed another statute that is also relevant.

To find cases related to the statutes that apply to your issue, click on "ORS Annotations" (currently, this appears in the left margin). While the ORS Annotations are not comprehensive, you might find a few cases that are on point or that will lead to other, relevant cases.

To determine if any regulations are on point, use the Oregon Secretary of State's website to access the Oregon Administrative Rules Database. You can search rule text using keywords in the Oregon Administrative Rules, or you can browse by chapter name if you know the name of the relevant administrative agency. Update administrative rules by using the link to the Oregon Bulletin on the Secretary of State's website. Administrative agency decisions may be available on individual agency websites.

D. Finding Cases

Google Scholar can be an effective tool for locating cases. From the home page, click on "Case law," and then select Oregon cases. Enter a natural language search using your issue statement in the search box, refining it based on what you have learned so far in your research. Using links in the left margin, limit the results by date, and sort results by relevance or date. Read the cases that seem relevant, noting that they may have star paging available only for the Pacific Reporter, not an official Oregon reporter. Although Google Scholar does not have headnotes for expanding your research, each case will have hyperlinks to other cases. You can expand your research using the "How cited" link that appears at the top left when you are viewing a case. In addition to conducting new research, you can try typing into the search bar the citation to cases you found in earlier steps.

Fastcase is free to Oregon Bar members and some law libraries provide access for their patrons. From the Fastcase start page, click on the "Jurisdictions" drop down arrow at the far right of the search bar. Set your search parameters selecting the jurisdictions you wish to search on the left-side box or select the sources you wish to search in the right-side box. After you select sources and jurisdictions, click on the save and continue button and then enter a search with keywords, natural language, or a citation.

E. Reading Cases

You can read cases in Google Scholar, find them on a court's website, or (for some physical activity) go to the library and pull volumes from the shelves. For older reporter volumes that are not on the shelves, ask at the circulation desk if the volumes are easy to retrieve from storage. Print or photocopy cases that seem especially important.

F. Updating Cases

Google Scholar provides a citator called "How cited," mentioned above for expanding your research. You could use it to begin the process of ensuring your case is still good law. However, to ensure the validity of cases and to check the validity of statutes, you should use KeyCite or Shepard's.

Fastcase has citator called "Cert Report," which is not as comprehensive as the citators provided by Lexis and Westlaw but will provide negative citations as well as other citations. Cert. Check does not have the same analytical tools and information as Shepard's and KeyCite, so you will have to do more close reading to understand how your case is being treated by other cases.

G. Ending Research

You can feel confident that your research is nearing an end when you begin to see the same sources cited repeatedly. That is, if the secondary sources all refer to the same key authorities, and your most important cases all cite the same statutes and each other, and all of the cases and statutes are good law, you have likely been thorough. Outline your analysis; if any holes remain — meaning that you are missing an analytical link or that you do not have support for a particular element or factor — return to the research process.

III. Using Lexis+ AI and Keyword Searching on Lexis

Table 11.2. Relevant Research Strategies using Lexis+AI

Use generative AI tools
Set search parameters
Use filters
Browse a table of contents
Search with a citation
Use statutory annotations
Search using natural language
Search using Boolean language
Expand research with a citator
Update with a citator

A. Conducting Pre-Research Tasks and Running the First Search

If you are having trouble framing an issue or want to brainstorm search terms, consider using Lexis's AI Assistant. On Lexis+ AI, you can "ask a legal question" to start generating ideas. Next to the "ask a legal question box," you can click on a link for "prompt tips." Also, consider prompting best practices introduced in Chapter 2. Your results will likely give you some leads to primary authority, as well as help you refine your search terms and research question.

After you've worked with the Lexis+ AI tools, move back to the Lexis platform, clarify your issue and generate search terms based on the facts and the research question. Consider carefully the terms likely to appear in relevant documents. If proximity of terms is important, create a search query with Boolean connectors to control the results; review search tips to ensure that you are using the correct connectors for this service.

Enter your search query in the universal search bar. Set the jurisdiction to Oregon and check the box to include non-jurisdictional content; Oregon is a small jurisdiction, so general secondary sources can provide useful background information. Do not yet limit by content (e.g., cases, statutes), or by practice area or topic. Your search results will be summarized by content in the left screen, divided by category of documents. Some of the categories are listed below:

- Cases,
- Statutes and Legislation,
- Practical Guidance,
- Secondary Materials,
- Administrative Materials,
- Briefs, Pleadings and Motions,
- Administrative Codes and Regulations,
- Sample Forms,
- Legal News,
- Jury Verdicts and Settlements, and
- Jury Instructions.

If you don't see a long list of content categories, look for "More" at the bottom of the list, and click on that link. The right screen will show the category of document you have set as your default under "Settings." If the default is not set to "Secondary Materials," you'll want to click on that link first.

B. Researching Secondary Sources

Review "Secondary Materials." Using the filters in the left margin, consider narrowing by jurisdiction, depending on the number of results returned. If you see many Oregon-specific sources, you might begin there, but be willing to move back to non-jurisdictional materials if you don't find helpful Oregon material. Decide which type of secondary source is most likely to be helpful for your project. If you need an authoritative overview, for example, begin with a treatise or practice guide. Alternatively, a database containing American Jurisprudence or American Law Reports could provide a less detailed explanation of the law, but more references to primary authorities in several jurisdictions. Because you are just beginning to research and this is a new area of law, do not start by looking at law review articles as they tend to be too specific. You might come back to these later if you need analysis of an open legal question or if you want to know how different jurisdictions interpret a certain law.

Work methodically through a few secondary sources that seem relevant. Skim the headings, and then read the text for those results that seem on point. Note potentially relevant statutes, regulations, and cases referenced in the text or in footnotes. Decide which documents to open or save to a folder. Some researchers like to open tabs for all possibly relevant statutes or cases until they have finished reading the treatise, and then read the opened authorities all together and save the relevant ones to a folder. Other researchers prefer to skim each statute or case as they encounter it, saving relevant ones to a folder. Briefly annotate or highlight each document so that when you return to it later you will remember why it seemed relevant.

C. Researching Enacted Law and Related Cases

Select the category "Statutes and Legislation." Filter the results by jurisdiction to only statutes from Oregon. If there are still too many for you to review, filter by search terms. A drop-down menu lets you search within your results to either include or exclude documents with certain words. You might first skim a few statutes in the results to determine which terms will filter the results list most effectively. For each entry in your filtered results list, read the title and the summary carefully. Determine whether the entry is a statute or an annotation to a case discussing a statute; focus first on statutes. When you find a relevant statute, read it carefully. Then read it again. Outline it to ensure you understand its parts. Read the statutory sections located before and after each relevant statute, browsing with the forward and backward arrows on the right and left sides of the actual document, or using the "Table of Contents" tab. Also read any statutes cross-referenced in a relevant statute; you can find them in the Table of Contents or by running a search for the citation.

To see how courts have interpreted and applied the statute, access and read the annotations. On the left side of the screen, choose Notes to Decisions. Realize that annotations might be numbered, or there might be an index of annotations, grouping them under related categories. These numbers and categories are not part of the statutory code, but research aids that can help you identify the most useful annotations for your project.

You might also use the citator, Shepard's, at this point, both to ensure that the statute is still current and to find more cases that have applied it. While you are looking at the document, click either on "Citing Decisions" at the top of the screen or on "Shepardize document" on the right side of the screen. You should expect overlap between cases you find in the Notes to Decisions for the statute and in Shepard's. This overlap should make you feel confident in your research; however, you should look carefully for cases included in one source but not the other.

Next, return to your initial search (click on "Back to Results" in the top left corner) and select "Administrative Codes and Regulations." Again, you might need to first click "More" to see that category listed. Review the results for the text of relevant regulations or agency action included in the Oregon Bulletin. Then select the category "Administrative Materials" for related agency decisions. Within each of these categories, you might use the "Sources" link on the left side of the screen to find the exact materials you are looking for (e.g., OR-Oregon Bulletin).

D. Finding Additional Cases

Return to your initial search (either using the "History" link at the top right of the screen or clicking back) and open the "Cases" category. Once again, narrow the results by using the filters in the left margin; with the research you have done so far, you should be able to filter effectively by court, search terms, date, etc. Your goal is to have a results list with a manageable number of cases that appear to be relevant. Don't filter so much, however, that you eliminate potentially relevant cases.

Two additional alternatives might also be effective in locating more cases. First, using the cases that you have determined are relevant, use the links in those headnotes to find more cases on relevant legal topics. Open a relevant case and use the list in the left margin to jump to its "Headnotes." Second, in a key case that you find, highlight relevant text and use the drop-down option to "Add to search"; this approach will locate additional cases that Lexis identifies as related to or similar to the text you selected.

E. Reading Cases

This is another step in which you might try generative AI tools. Access Lexis+ AI Assistant on the top left side of the Lexis start page; one option is to ask AI Assistant to summarize a case. This might be a good step when you are just starting research to be more efficient in deciding which cases might be the best to investigate further. However, never rely on a case that you have not fully read and analyzed yourself.

When you decide on the cases you want to read, you will go beyond the quick skimming you have done in the earlier steps of the research process. Now, you must read each potentially relevant case very closely, understand how it affects your client's issue, and decide whether it should be part of your analysis. Begin by reading the synopsis of each case to get an overview. Then, read the headnotes to determine the significant portions of the case (because if one portion does not contain your search terms, it will not have been highlighted from the word search but might still be significant). Jump from possibly relevant headnotes to the linked portion of the case, reading that portion carefully to determine its impact on your project. Additionally, the ribbon in the left margin that is green will identify those parts of the case that contain more of your search terms, which may be good places to begin.

Read each relevant case in full at least once. After deciding that a few paragraphs or a few pages of a case discuss an unimportant procedural issue or another cause of action, you can avoid those pages in future readings. Consider crossing them out on printed pages or annotating them online.

When you decide a case is relevant, quickly check its Shepard's status to ensure that the portion you plan to rely on is still good law.

F. Using Shepard's

As noted above, you should have been glancing at the Shepard's symbols on statutes and cases to determine whether they have negative or pending treatment. An explanation of symbols is linked to the "Legend" that appears on each page in Shepard's. Some of the more common symbols are discussed in Chapter 3, Part III.C.4 of this book.

Now you have three more tasks to complete for each case you intend to rely on. First, click on "Shepardize document" on the right side of the page. Then, ensure that your case is still good law by using the tab for "History." Remember that you can Shepardize using headnotes so that you validate only the portion of the case that is relevant to your work, saving you time. Next, check the "Table of Authorities" for hidden weaknesses. If the key cases that your case relied on have a long line of negative treatment, your case may no longer be based on good law. Moreover, because the Table of Authorities lists each case cited by the case you are Shepardizing, you might skim it for additional cases to read.

Third, expand your research with the tab for "Citing Decisions." If there are many citing decisions, use the filters to restrict to a reasonable number of recent cases from your jurisdiction that discuss similar facts. Your goal here is to find additional cases that might be even more important than those you found earlier in the process. Be sure not to disregard a case with negative facts or negative analysis for the outcome your client desires; you will have to address those weaknesses.

G. Ending Research

You can be confident in your research when you begin to see the same relevant sources come up repeatedly and when you can complete your analysis with the authorities you have found.

IV. Using Natural and Boolean Language Searches on Westlaw

Table 11.3. Relevant Research Strategies using Westlaw

Use generative AI tools
Set search parameters
Use filters
Use topic searching
Use statutory annotations
Search using Boolean language
Expand research with a citator
Update with a citator

A. Conducting Pre-Research Tasks

Before opening Westlaw, complete the following pre-research tasks:

- Gather facts,
- Determine the issue,
- Decide which jurisdiction controls,
- Generate a list of research terms,
- Create different types of searches, and
- Set up folders online or create a research log on which to record and organize your results.

Often the pre-research tasks are intertwined. You might gather facts from several sources, including a client interview, a memo from your supervisor, documents between the parties (e.g., contracts or letters), and interviews with witnesses. Those facts might make clear what the legal issue is, especially if a supervisor tells you to research a particular cause of action; on the other hand, you might need to do preliminary research to determine which issues might be in play. The facts and issues will impact the jurisdiction, and sometimes a legal problem might include aspects of state and federal law. For purposes of this explanation, assume that you are researching Oregon law.

From the facts and issue, develop a list of search terms, as explained in Chapter 2. Next, using those terms, create searches. If this is a completely unfamiliar area of law, you might begin with natural language searches. These searches simply ask a question (is a noncompete clause enforceable in Oregon?), state a phrase (negligent infliction of emotional distress), or include relevant terms (statute of limitations for property disputes). If you are familiar with the issue, or if other searches are returning irrelevant material, try creating Boolean searches using terms and connectors. Decide which proximity connectors (e.g., /3, /s, /p) will be most useful, considering whether these terms will likely appear in helpful documents within a few words of each other, in the same sentence, or in the same paragraph. Then, decide which databases are likely to contain your target documents. In researching an Oregon state law issue, review the sources under links to "State Materials" and "Oregon," some of which are listed below:

- Cases,
- All Oregon State & Federal Cases,
- Oregon Supreme Court,
- Oregon Court of Appeals,
- Oregon Tax Court,
- Statutes & Court Rules,
- Oregon Statutes & Court Rules,
- Oregon Rules of Civil Procedure,
- Oregon Rules of Evidence,
- Regulations,
- Oregon Regulations,
- Administrative Decisions & Guidance,
- Oregon Administrative Decisions & Guidance,
- Secondary Sources,
- All Oregon Secondary Sources,

- Oregon Law & Practice,
- Oregon State Bar Bulletin,
- Willamette Law Review, and
- Oregon Employment Law Letter.

Select appropriate databases for each step of the research process. Think critically about whether to use a general or specific database. You might decide to begin searching general secondary sources, as there are few specifically on Oregon law. Then you might decide to search only Oregon Supreme Court and Court of Appeals cases, excluding cases from federal courts or the Oregon Tax Court.

Finally, create a folder in Westlaw where you will keep documents related to this research project. Either now, or as the need arises during your research, create subfolders. The subfolders could be based on different issues (e.g., if you have two tort claims and a related contracts claim), on the components of a single claim (e.g., the elements of negligence), or on general divisions that make sense to you (e.g., primary authority, secondary authority).

B. Researching Secondary Sources

From "Content types," below the universal search bar, select "Secondary Sources." Because you are researching in an area of law that is new to you, consider selecting "Texts & Treatises." You can search across all the publications under that category, you can narrow to a subset of Texts & Treatises such as "Jurisprudence & Encyclopedias," or you can narrow to a single publication (e.g., "American Jurisprudence 2d"). When you select a category or a specific publication, that will appear to the left of the universal search bar.

Enter your Boolean search query in the universal search bar. If you receive many results, use the tools in the left margin to filter your search results. Skim each document in the narrowed results list, reading the title and then the excerpt provided to determine whether it seems relevant.

Look carefully at footnotes, where you are most likely to find references to cases. If a source seems relevant, annotate it briefly to state how it applies and save it to your folder. Some researchers have a folder for sources that are not helpful, on which they note why the sources are not helpful to ensure they don't waste further time on them.

If you are finding nothing relevant, revise your search query or look in a different source. As examples, you might move from an encyclopedia to a treatise, or if you started in an Oregon-specific treatise, you might move to a general treatise. After skimming some sources, stop to read in-depth the most relevant secondary sources. Note any references to primary authorities that you should read. Continue working with secondary sources until you begin to understand the area of law and perhaps have citations to a few relevant cases or statutes.

C. Researching Enacted Law and Related Cases

If the secondary source referred to a relevant constitutional provision or statute, read it immediately. But also conduct independent research to ensure that you have not overlooked another relevant provision or statute. Open an Oregon statutes database, remembering that you can access it in several ways:

1. Type *Oregon statutes* into the universal search bar,
2. Browse under "Content types" for "Statutes & Court Rules" then "Oregon," or
3. Browse under "State Materials" and "Oregon," and then "Oregon Statutes & Court Rules."

Enter your Boolean search query in the universal search bar, realizing that you might want to refine it after your work in secondary sources. Skim the research results. Most likely, they will not contain relevant constitutional provisions. They will likely include both statutes and notes of decisions but focus first on those that refer to statutes. Once you have identified a relevant statute, read it carefully at least twice. Outline it, especially if it is long or complex, breaking it into manageable bullet points. Read any statutes that it references. Click on "Table of Contents" to see whether other nearby statutes are also relevant. Check any KeyCite indicator to ensure that the statute is current and has no negative treatment by cases in your jurisdiction. If you don't find any relevant statutes, modify your search query. If you still don't find anything, consider the possibility that the area is controlled by common law.

If you do find a relevant statute, open the "Notes of Decisions" from the link at the top of the screen or the box under the statutory text. If there are many cases indexed with this statute, you might be able to narrow your search using a list of subheadings. Skim the notes for relevant cases. Even if all the cases in "Notes of Decisions" seem dated, you can use them as a springboard to other research by using their Topics and Key Numbers in the West Topic and Key Number system or by using KeyCite. Save the relevant statute(s) and cases to your folder. If you haven't found many helpful cases in Notes of Decisions, you can also expand your research by using KeyCite's link to "Citing References" and the subcategory "Cases."

At this point, consider researching administrative law to see if an agency has issued regulations that might affect your issue. If so, it might add further to your understanding of the related statute, and agency decisions might have applied the statute and regulations in particular situations. Your research might already have revealed relevant regulations: they might have been mentioned in a secondary source, annotations to a statute, or related cases. To conduct a fresh search, type Oregon regulations in the universal search bar or browse below the search bar for databases with Oregon state regulations (e.g., State Materials > Oregon > Oregon Regulations). Continue with the detailed instructions provided in Chapter 8.

D. Finding Cases with the Topic and Key Number System

Although you might have already found several cases from secondary sources and annotated statutes, you should still use the Topic and Key Number system to expand your research. Note that if your research issue is controlled by common law, you will not find a statute, regulations, or related annotations, and Topic and Key Number research will be even more important.

Using "Content types," click on "Topics & Key Numbers." Select Oregon as your jurisdiction to narrow the results. Either search for your terms using the box at the top of the page or skim the list of Topics and expand relevant headings by clicking on the Topic name. You can click on the small "i" icon next to a Topic's name to learn what it covers as well as suggestions for other Topics that might be more relevant. The results of your search will be a list of headnotes from cases that West has indexed under a particular Topic and Key Number. Skim the headnotes and determine which cases are relevant. Annotate those and save them to your folder. Remember that an eyeglasses icon means that you have already viewed a document. If you begin to see the same relevant cases repeatedly, you should feel good about the effectiveness of your research.

E. Reading Cases

By this point, your folder should have several cases that you have determined are relevant. Take time to read each one carefully, using the techniques explained in Chapter 1. If you determine a case is not relevant, add an annotation to the first page of the case briefly stating why and move it to another folder. Keeping a folder of discarded cases can help you avoid rereading cases later that you have already determined are not useful. Some people like to print the most relevant cases because reading in print could help with concentration on the text and can facilitate making more comprehensive annotations to the case.

F. Using KeyCite

As you encountered each statute, regulation, or case that you thought was relevant, you should have quickly checked to see whether it had a red or yellow symbol indicating negative treatment that could affect that authority's impact on your analysis. Now, for each case that you have tentatively decided to rely on, use KeyCite to ensure that the case is still good law. Check the "History" and "Negative Treatment" as well as the "Table of Authorities" (if other authorities that this case relied on are no longer valid, this case's analysis might not be either). Then expand your research by clicking on "Citing References." You might find additional cases that are more recent, that have clearer analyses, or that have facts closer to your client's situation.

G. Ending Research

When you have completed each step of the process and you have begun to see the same relevant sources appear in various steps, you might be nearing the end of your research. Sketch an outline of the elements or key arguments, and see whether you have sufficient statutory, administrative, or case law to support each. If not, continue research, trying new sources and new search terms. If so, move into organizing your analysis for either a final document or an oral presentation.

V. Conclusion

Like most skills, legal research improves with practice. Try to view each frustrating experience with a search engine or resource as an opportunity to learn more about the research process. Most of all, remember that professional reference librarians are available to assist you, whether you are a novice or an experienced researcher.

Appendix A

Legal Citation

I. Purposes of Legal Citation

Table A.1. Purposes of Legal Citation

1. Instruct the reader how to locate the source
2. Identify the weight of the source
3. Communicate the type of support for a statement or assertion
4. Document the thoroughness of research

When writing about legal research and analysis, lawyers use legal citations to refer to the authorities used to develop that analysis and reach the conclusion. Legal citations tell readers where to find the authorities relied on. Legal citations also indicate the level of analytical support the authorities provide, whether those authorities support an idea directly or by inference and whether the authorities are from the controlling jurisdiction.

In a legal document, every legal rule and every explanation of the law must be cited. Legal citations are included in the text of legal documents rather than being saved for a bibliography. To minimize the space devoted to citations, lawyers use abbreviations and formatting conventions that are generally well known. Consistent citation format within a document makes reading and understanding citations easy. While many different citation systems exist, they tend to follow well established formats and conventions. Table A.1 lists the purposes of legal citation.

II. Steps for Drafting Citations

Like research, drafting legal citations takes practice. Until you develop expertise in citation forms, following structured steps will be helpful (see Table A.2).

Table A.2. Steps to Draft Accurate Citations

1. Identify the type of source (statute, administrative rule, case, etc.).
2. Locate the relevant rule for that source in Oregon citation rules, *ALWD*, and *Bluebook* using indexes, tables of contents, etc.
3. Cite the official source rather than unofficial source, if available.
4. Use *ALWD* appendices or *Bluebook* tables for abbreviations.
5. Follow typeface and capitalization requirements in *ALWD* Rules 1 and 3 or *Bluebook* Blue Pages, B4.
6. Use short form rules as stated in *ALWD* Rule 11 or *Bluebook* Blue Pages, B4.
7. Edit citations—check rules while first drafting the citation, then review and edit after you have finished writing your document.

III. Sources for Citation Rules

There are several sources for citations rules. Table A.3. lists the sources you will need to correctly cite in Oregon.

Table A.3. Sources for Citation Rules

Source	Examples	Explanation
Oregon Citation Rules • Uniform Trial Court Rules • Oregon Appellate Courts Style Manual	ORS 164.225	Abbreviation for *Oregon Revised Statutes*, statute number
	Hoffman v. Freeman Land and Timber, LLC., 329 Or 554 (1999) *State v. Reid*, 36 Or App 417 (1978). *Linder v. Dept. of Rev.*, 18 OTR 11 (2004). *Brown v. Bd. Of Educ.*, 349 US 294 (1955).	Name of parties, reporter volume number, reporter abbreviation, first page of case, date.
	OAR 808-003-0010.	Oregon Administrative Rules abbreviation, rule number
	ORCP 71 B (1)(b).	Oregon Rules of Civil Procedure abbreviation, rule number
Bluebook • Reference Guide inside back cover • Bluepages • Index	Or. Rev. Stat. § 164.225 (2021)	National citation manual abbreviation for *Oregon Revised Statutes*, statute number, year
ALWD • Fast Formats • Table of Contents • Index	*Hoffman v. Freeman Land and Timber, LLC.*, 329 Or. 554 (1999). *State v. Reid*, 36 Or. App. 417 (1978).	National citation manual reporter abbreviations include periods

A. Oregon Citation Rules Essentials

In Oregon, two sources of citation rules are the Uniform Trial Court Rules (UTCR) and the Oregon Appellate Courts Style Manual (OSM). Under these rules, no periods are used in reporter abbreviations. To illustrate, Oregon Reports and Oregon Reports, Court of Appeals are abbreviated "Or" and "Or App" without punctuation. When citing *Oregon Revised Statutes* while working in Oregon, use the abbreviation "ORS." Do not include the date when referring to the current code. After using an online service or *West's Oregon Revised Statutes Annotated* (WORSA) to conduct your research, you might quickly confirm the statutory language in ORS and cite to that official source.

The OSM includes examples of citations for constitutions, legislative material, rules of civil procedure and evidence, administrative rules, and much more. It also contains a writing style guide that addresses such things as capitalization, punctuation, word usage, and parallel construction. The OSM is available online from the Oregon Judicial Department links.

B. National Citation Manuals

While state citation rules often provide only rules and examples, national citation manuals also attempt to explain in some detail the components of citations. The two national citation manuals that are currently popular are the *Bluebook* and the ALWD Guide. The content and format of citations produced by the two manuals is almost always identical; however, different typeface is required for citations in practice documents and for footnotes in law review articles. The biggest difference for the student is that the ALWD Guide focuses its examples and explanations on the style of citation used in legal memoranda and briefs, while the *Bluebook*'s focus is on citation format used in law review articles and other academic publications.

1. *Bluebook* Essentials

Student editors of four Ivy League law reviews developed the citation rules in the *Bluebook*. The Oregon Appellate Courts Style Manual defers to the *Bluebook* for rules not covered in the state manual. Many law firms, agencies, and organizations consider *Bluebook* citations the norm; it is the oldest citation manual still in general use. Although the rules change with each new edition, most attorneys assume that the *Bluebook* has not changed since they were in law school.

For practicing attorneys, the primary difficulty with the *Bluebook* is that its focus is on the citation style used in law review articles, not the format used for legal memoranda and court documents. Because most of the *Bluebook* examples are in law review format, a student or lawyer using the *Bluebook* must translate each example into the format used in legal practice documents.

Perhaps the most helpful information in the *Bluebook* is the reference guide on the inside back cover of the book, which gives examples of citations used in court documents and legal memoranda. Another helpful section is the "Bluepages" at the beginning of the book. This section provides information for, and additional examples of citations used in documents other than law review articles.

The index at the back of the *Bluebook* is quite extensive, and in most instances is more helpful than the table of contents. Most often, you should begin working by referring to the index. Note that the references in the index are to page numbers, not rule numbers. Blue-bordered pages at the back contain tables with jurisdictional material (federal and states), and abbreviations for case names, courts, and law journals.

2. ALWD Essentials

The Association of Legal Writing Directors (ALWD) publishes a citation manual that is intended to make citation instruction straightforward. Both the instructions and the examples focus on the citations used in legal practice; an alternate format for academic citations is designated "Academic Formatting."

Three finding tools lead to relevant rules in the *ALWD Guide*:

- The table of contents outlining the organization of the rules in the guide;
- The index at the back of the guide; and
- Tables of "Fast Formats," at the beginning of sections on specific sources, referring to example citations.

In the guide's index, most references are to rules or to specific sidebars, charts, appendices, or other features. Appendix 1 at the back of the guide lists abbreviations for primary sources of law for each state, presented alphabetically, along with resources for federal, Native American, and territorial law. For Oregon, this appendix includes abbreviations for state and regional reporters, state statutes and regulations, the state constitution, etc. Appendix 3E gives abbreviations to use for case names in citations, and Appendix 4 provides abbreviations for courts. Appendix 5, which includes abbreviations for law journals, is available online.

IV. Noteworthy Citation Formats

A. Citing Oregon Materials with National Citation Formats

Because the *ALWD Guide* and the *Bluebook* are designed for national use, they use different abbreviations for some Oregon materials. The most obvious difference is that *Oregon Revised Statutes* is abbreviated "Or. Rev. Stat." instead of "ORS" because an attorney working outside of Oregon would not be expected to know whether ORS referred to the statutes of Ohio, Oklahoma, or Oregon. The longer abbreviation provides clarity.

Another small difference is that, in the national manuals, all reporter abbreviations include periods. Thus, the Oregon reporters are abbreviated "Or." for Oregon Reports and "Or. App." for Oregon Reports, Court of Appeals. Similarly, Pacific Reporter, Third Series would be abbreviated "P.3d" rather than "P3d" (as under Oregon rules).

B. Incorporating Citations into a Legal Document

Table A.4. Examples of Citation Sentences and Citation Clauses

Citation Sentences: First-degree burglary involves a building that is a dwelling. Or. Rev. Stat. § 164.225 (2021). The term dwelling is defined as "a building which regularly or intermittently is occupied by a person lodging therein at night, whether or not a person is actually present." Or. Rev. Stat. § 164.205(2) (2021).
Citation Clauses: Oregon statutes define both first-degree burglary, Or. Rev. Stat. § 164.225 (2021), and second-degree burglary, Or. Rev. Stat. § 164.215 (2021).

A legal document must provide a citation for each idea that comes from a case, statute, article, or other source. So, paragraphs that state legal rules and explain the law should contain many citations.

A citation may offer support for an entire sentence or for an idea expressed in part of a sentence. If the citation supports the entire sentence, it is placed in a separate citation sentence that begins with a capital letter and ends with a period. If the citation supports only a portion of the sentence, it is included immediately after the relevant part of that sentence and is set off from the sentence by commas in what is called a citation clause. *Bluebook* Bluepages B1.1 and *ALWD* Rule 34 provide examples.

Cite all sentences that contain legal rules or that explain legal rules. Do not cite your client's facts to a legal authority, and do not cite your unique conclusions about a legal authority. The following sentence should not be cited: "Under the facts presented, our client's conduct would fall under first-degree burglary because a homeless family sometimes slept in the building she broke into." These facts and conclusions are unique to your situation. Table A.4 provides examples of how to incorporate citations.

C. Statutory Citations

Table A.5. Oregon Appellate Courts Style Manual

Narrative form examples		Citation form examples	
ORS chapter 554	When referring to entire chapter	ORS ch 554	When citing an entire chapter
ORS 30.150 to 30.175; ORS 250.035(2)(a) to (c)	When referring to a statutory sequence	ORS 30.150–30.175; ORS 250.035(2)(a)–(c)	When citing a statutory sequence
ORS 30.866 and ORS 163.730	When referring to two statutes	ORS 30.866; ORS 163.730	When citing two statutes
ORS 250.035(2)(a) and (b)	When referring to two parts of the same statute	ORS 250.035(2)(a), (b)	When citing two parts of the same statute

The Oregon Appellate Courts Style Manual requires the use of the abbreviation ORS for the *Oregon Revised Statutes*. When citing an Oregon statute in a court outside of Oregon, use the *Bluebook* citation form as explained in Bluepages, Rule B12.1.2 and Table T1.3 which lists the official and unofficial statutory compilations of each state. (See Table A.5.)

D. Case Citations

Table A.6. Example Case Citations

1. *Glik v. Cunniffe*, 655 F.3d 78, 80 (1st Cir. 2011).
2. *Citizens United v. Fed. Election Comm'n*, 558 U.S. 310, 340 (2010).
3. *Mid-Valley Res., Inc. v. Engelson*, 170 Or. App. 255, 259 (2000).
4. *Ketchum v. Moses*, 17 P.3d 735, 736 (Cal. 2001).

Detailed rules for case citation are included in Rule 10 of the *Bluebook* and Rule 12 of the *ALWD Guide*. A full citation to a case includes (1) the name of the case, (2) the volume and reporter in which the case is published, (3) the first page of the case, (4) the exact page in the case that contains the idea you are citing (i.e., the pinpoint or jump cite), (5) an abbreviation for the court that decided the case, and (6) the date the case was decided.

1. Name of the Case

Include the name of just the first party on each side, even if several are listed in the case caption. If the party is an individual, include only the party's family name. If the party is a business or organization, shorten the party's name by using the abbreviations (such as Inc. and Co.) provided by the citation manuals. Between the parties' names, place a lower case "v" followed by a period. Do not use a capital "V" or the abbreviation "vs." Place a comma after the second party's name; do not italicize or underline this comma. The parties' names may be italicized or underlined. Use the style preferred by your supervisor and use that style consistently throughout each document. Do not combine italics and underlining in one cite or within a single document.

2. Volume and Reporter

Next, give the volume and the abbreviation for the reporter in which the case is found. Pay special attention to whether the reporter is in its first, second, or third series. In example 1 above, the *Glik* case, 655 is the volume number and F.3d is the reporter abbreviation for Federal Reporter, Third Series. After the reporter name, include both the first page of the case and the pinpoint page containing the idea that you are referencing, separated by a comma and a space. The first page of the *Glik* case above is 78, and the page containing the specific idea being cited is 80. If the pinpoint page you are citing is also the first page of the case, then the same page number will appear twice.

3. Court Abbreviation

In a parenthetical following this information, indicate the court that decided the case, using abbreviations provided by the manual. The *ALWD Guide* and the *Bluebook* both have a list of state and federal courts and their citation abbreviations. In the *Glik* example, the First Circuit Court of Appeals, a federal court, decided the case.

If the reporter abbreviation clearly indicates which court decided a case, do not repeat this information in the parenthetical. To give two examples, only cases of the United States Supreme Court are reported in *United States Reports*, abbreviated U.S. (see example 2 above). Only cases decided by the Oregon Court of Appeals are reported in *Oregon Reports, Court of Appeals*, abbreviated Or. App (see example 3 above). Repeating court abbreviations in citations to those reporters would be duplicative. By contrast, *Pacific Reporter, Third Series*, abbreviated P.3d, publishes decisions from different courts within several states, so the court that decided a particular case needs to be indicated parenthetically. In example 4 above, "Cal." indicates that the decision came from the California Supreme Court rather than from another court whose decisions are also published in the P.3d reporter.

The final piece of required information in most cites is the date the case was decided. For cases published in reporters, give only the year of decision, not the month or date. Do not confuse the date of decision with the date on which the case was argued or submitted, the date on which a motion for rehearing was denied, or the publication date of the reporter. For cases available only online, give the month abbreviation, date, and year.

4. Full and Short Citations to Cases

Table A.7. Example of Full and Short Citations

Open and notorious possession requires the claimants to prove the owners had notice that the claimants were asserting title to the disputed property. *Slak v. Porter*, 128 Or. App. 274, 278 (1994). The notice may be actual or constructive. *Id.* at 279. Owners have actual notice when they are aware that their claim of the land is being challenged. *See id.* Constructive notice is satisfied when claimants use the property in a manner considered to give the owner knowledge of their use and claim. *Hoffman v. Freeman Land and Timber, LLC.*, 329 Or. 554, 559 (1999). Construction of a fence is the classic example of open and notorious possession. *Slak*, 128 Or. App. at 279.

The first time you mention a case by name, immediately give its full citation, including all the information outlined above. After using a full citation once to introduce an authority, use short citations to cite to this same authority. A short citation provides just enough information to allow the reader to locate the longer citation and find the pin-point page.

When the immediately preceding cite is to the same source and the same page, use *id.* as the short cite. When the second cite is to a different page within the same source, follow the *id.* with "at" and the new pinpoint page number. Capitalize *id.* when it begins a citation sentence, just as the beginning of any sentence is capitalized. Note that the short cite *id.* can be used only when the preceding citation is to a single authority.

If the immediately preceding cite is to a different source, give the name of one of the parties, the volume, the reporter, and the pinpoint page following "at." In general, use the name of the first party in the full cite; if that party is "United States," a state, or another common litigant, use the opposing party's name. Signals like *see* are explained below.

If you refer to the case by name in the sentence, your short citation does not need to repeat the case name, although lawyers often do. The last sentence of the example would also be correct as follows: In *Slak*, construction of a fence was recognized as the classic example of open and notorious possession. 128 Or. App. at 279. The format, *Slak* at 279, consisting of just a case name and page number, is incorrect. The volume and reporter abbreviation are also needed. See Table A.7 for examples.

5. Prior and Subsequent History

Table A.8. Example of Citing History

The Supreme Court has upheld the right to marry as a fundamental right. *Obergefell v. Hodges*, 576 U.S. 644 (2015), *rev'g DeBoer v. Snyder*, 772 F.3d 388 (6th Cir. 2014).

Sometimes a citation needs to show what happened to a case at an earlier or later stage of litigation. The case you are citing may have reversed an earlier case (Table A.8 shows an example). If you are citing a case for a court's analysis of one issue and a later court reversed only on another issue, you need to alert your reader to that reversal. Or, if you decide for historical purposes to include in a document discussion of a case that was later overruled, your reader needs to know that as soon as you introduce the case. Prior and subsequent history can be appended to the full citations discussed above; the history begins with an italicized abbreviation like *rev'g* (for reversing a prior case) or *aff'd* (when the case was affirmed).

E. Signals

A citation must show the level of support each authority provides. You do this by deciding whether to use an introductory signal and, if so, which one. The more common signals are explained in Table A.9.

Table A.9. Common Signals

No Signal	The source cited provides direct support for the idea in the sentence; or The cite identifies the source of the quotation.
See	The source cited offers implicit support for the idea in the sentence.
See also	The source cited provides additional support for the idea in the sentence. (The support offered by *see also* is not as strong or direct as authorities preceded by no signal or by the signal *see*).
E.g.,	Many authorities state the idea in the sentence, and you are citing only one as an example; this signal allows you to cite just one source while letting the reader know that many other sources say the same thing.

F. Parentheticals

Table A.10. Example of an Explanatory Parenthetical

Before striking a contradictory affidavit under the "sham affidavit rule," a court must find the inconsistency between the party's deposition and subsequent affidavit to be "clear and unambiguous." *Van Asdale v. Int'l Game Tech.*, 577 F.3d 989, 998–99 (9th Cir. 2009) (urging district courts to apply the "sham affidavit rule" with caution).

At the end of a cite, you can append additional information about the authority in parentheses. (See Table A.10.) Sometimes this parenthetical information conveys to the reader the weight of the authority. For example, a case may have been decided *en banc* (heard by all the judges, rather than a panel) or *per curiam* (decided by the whole court, without a named author). Or the case may have been decided by a narrow split among the judges who heard the case. Parenthetical information also allows you to name the judges who joined in a dissenting, concurring, or plurality opinion. An explanatory parenthetical following a signal can convey helpful, additional information in a compressed space. Parenthetical information generally should not be given in a complete sentence, but should begin with a present participle (i.e., a verb ending in "-ing") that is not capitalized. When using this type of parenthetical, be sure that you do not inadvertently hide a critical part of the court's analysis at the end of a long citation, where a reader is likely to skip over it.

G. Quotations

Table A.11. Quotation Example

Original Statutory Text: In the case of a hospital that has a hospital emergency department, if any individual (whether or not eligible for benefits under this subchapter) comes to the emergency department and a request is made on the individual's behalf for examination or treatment for a medical condition, the hospital must provide for an appropriate medical screening examination within the capability of the hospital's emergency department, including ancillary services routinely available to the emergency department, to determine whether or not an emergency medical condition (within the meaning of subsection (e)(1)) exists. 42 U.S.C. § 1395dd(a).
Quotation in Appellate Brief: A hospital with an emergency room must provide every patient with "an appropriate medical screening examination within the capability of the hospital's emergency department ... to determine whether or not an emergency medical condition ... exists." 42 U.S.C. § 1395dd(a).

Use quotations only when the reader needs to see the text exactly as it appears in the original authority. Of all legal audiences, trial courts are probably most receptive to longer quotations. For example, quoting the controlling statutory language can be extremely helpful. Or, if a well-known case explains an analytical point in a particularly insightful way, a quotation may be warranted.

Excessive quotation has two drawbacks. First, quotations interrupt the flow of your writing when the style of the quoted language differs from your own.

> EXAMPLE: The Ninth Circuit held that Oregon's Measure 11 did not violate constitutional rights provided under the Eighth and Fourteenth Amendments. *Alvarado v. Hill*, 252 F.3d 1066, 1069–70 (9th Cir. 2001).

Second, excessive use of quotations may suggest to the reader that you do not comprehend the material; it is much easier to cut and paste together a document from pieces of various cases than to synthesize and explain a rule of law.

Do not use quotations simply because you cannot think quickly of another way to express an idea.

When a quotation is warranted, the words, punctuation, and capitalization within the quotation marks must appear exactly as they are in the original. Treat a quotation as a photocopy or scan of the original text; indicate any alterations or omissions by using brackets or ellipses. Include commas and periods inside quotation marks; place other punctuation outside the quotation marks unless it is included in the original text. Also, try to provide smooth transitions between your text and the quoted text. Quotations that have fifty or more words must be set off in indented blocks.

H. Other Citation Notes

1. Use proper ordinal abbreviations. The most confusing are 2d for "Second" and 3d for "Third" because they differ from the standard format.
2. Do not use superscript for ordinal abbreviations. The abbreviation 4th is correct, while the abbreviation 4th is not.
3. Include space only between elements of abbreviations that are not single capital letters. As examples, there is no space in the reporter abbreviation "U.S.," but there is space in the federal district court designation "D. Or." and the law journal "Animal L."
4. Ordinal numbers like 1st, 2d, and 3d are considered single capital letters for abbreviation spacing. Thus, there is no space in P.2d or F.3d, but F. Supp. 2d has a space on each side of "Supp."
5. In citation sentences, abbreviate case names, court names, months, and reporter names. Do not abbreviate these words when they are part of textual sentences; instead, spell them out as in the example below.

6. When *id.* is used to show support for just part of a sentence, this short cite is set off from the sentence by commas and is not capitalized.
7. Spell out numbers zero through ninety-nine and use numerals for larger numbers. However, always spell out a number that is the first word of a sentence.

V. Citations for Law Review Articles

Table A.12. Typeface for Law Review Footnotes

Item	Example	Explanation
Case	Legal Servs. Corp v. Velazquez, 531 U.S. 533 (2001).	Use ordinary type for case names in full citations. (See below for further explanation.)
Book	MEGAN MCALPIN, BEYOND THE FIRST DRAFT: EDITING STRATEGIES FOR POWERFUL LEGAL WRITING (2014).	Use large and small capital letters for the author and title.
Law review article	Adell Louise Amos, *The Use of State Instream Flow Laws for Federal Land: Respecting State Control While Meeting Federal Purposes*, 36 ENVTL. L. 1237 (2006).	Use ordinary type for the author's name, italics for the title, and large and small capitals for the periodical.
Explanatory phrase	Legal Servs. Corp. v. Velazquez, 531 U.S. 533 (2001), *aff'g* 164 F.3d 757 (2d Cir. 1999).	Use italics for all explanatory phrases, such as *aff'g*, *cert. denied*, *rev'd*, and *overruled by*.
Introductory signal	*See id.*	Use italics for all introductory signals, such as *see* and *e.g.* when they appear in citations, as opposed to text.

Under the *ALWD Guide* and the *Bluebook*, citations in law review articles use different formatting than is used for practice documents. Using the *Bluebook* to write citations for law review articles is considerably easier than using it for practice documents. As noted in Table A.12, almost all the examples given in the *Bluebook* are in law review format.

Law review articles place citations in footnotes or endnotes, instead of placing citations in the main text of the document. Most law review footnotes include text in ordinary type (called *roman*), in italics, and in large and small capital letters, as shown in examples above. This convention is not universal, and each law review selects the typefaces it will use. Some law reviews may use only ordinary type and italics. Others may use just ordinary type.

The typeface used for a case name depends on (1) whether the case appears in the main text of the article or in a footnote and (2) how the case is used. When a case name appears in the main text of the article or in a textual sentence of a footnote, it is italicized. By contrast, when a full cite is given in a citation sentence in a footnote, the case name is written in ordinary type. But when a short cite is used in footnotes, the case name is italicized. Assuming you are submitting an article to a law review that uses all three typefaces, *ALWD* Rule 1 and *Bluebook* Rule 2 dictate which typeface to use for each type of authority.

Law review footnotes use short cites generally the same as in other documents. Remember that the short cite *id.* can be used only if the preceding footnote contains only one authority.

VI. Resources to Help with Citation

You may wish to consult several types of resources to aid in creating accurate citations. You should always check citations several times during the drafting process to ensure accuracy.

A. Books and Manuals

Several books can assist you with using citation manuals. You might find these books in an academic law library in print or ebook format: *Cite-Checker: Your Guide to Using the Bluebook*, 5th ed. by Deborah Bouchoux; *Interactive Citation Workbook for the Bluebook*, by Tracy L. McGaugh; Christine Hurt; and *Legal Writing Citation in a Nutshell*, by Larry Teply.

B. Research Platforms

Several research platforms have tools that can assist you with citation format.

1. Lexis

On Lexis, when you are looking at a resource such as a case, statute, or administrative rule, look at the top of the screen near the title of the resource to find the "copy citation" link. You can choose the citation style (standard aligns with *Bluebook* style), and then copy and paste it into your document. Also, you can select and copy text from a resource, copy that selection with a citation style you have previously selected, then paste that into your document.

2. Westlaw

Similarly, on Westlaw, when you are looking at a resource such as a case or statute, look in the upper right corner for the link icon. If you click on the down arrow next to the icon, you will see options to copy the link to the document, copy the citation, or copy the citation to an outline. You can choose the citation format and then paste that citation into the document you are drafting. Also, you can select text from the source and then choose to copy with citation to your document.

3. HeinOnline

If you are looking at a law journal article on HeinOnline, you can use the Cite button in the upper left side of the screen, choose the citation format, and copy and paste the citation into your document.

C. Citation Management Systems

Your academic institution may provide access to citation management systems that can generate citations in various formats. Examples of citation management systems are Mendeley, Zotero, Endnote, Refworks, and LegalEase.

Bestlaw is a free browser extension that you can use with Westlaw and Lexis to generate *Bluebook* citations. Citeus Legalus is a free citation generator.

Appendix B

Federal Research

The legal research process and the techniques discussed throughout this book are effective in researching federal law as well as Oregon law. This appendix introduces the sources of federal law (see Table B.1).

Table B.1. Federal Legal Sources

United States Constitution
Federal Statutes and Legislative History
Federal Court Rules
Federal Administrative Regulations and Agency Decisions
Federal Court Cases

I. United States Constitution

The federal constitution is widely available online and in print; each publication offers something unique. For example, the United States Senate's website includes two annotated versions, one of which provides a brief introduction and an explanation of each article and amendment to the constitution. Lexis and Westlaw provide the federal constitution and make it easy for researchers to find related cases, treatises, and other sources that interpret and explain the provisions. In print, the federal constitution is published along with the Oregon Constitution in *Oregon Revised Statutes* and in *West's Oregon Revised Statutes Annotated.* There is an index immediately following the federal constitution, and annotations are provided just as they are for statutes. The federal constitution is also available in print in the first few volumes of two commercial publications of federal statutes, United States Code Service (USCS) and United States Code Annotated (USCA), as a convenience for readers. These series are explained in the next part of this appendix. Many books, law review articles, and judicial opinions have been devoted to interpretation of the federal constitution. Refer to discussions in other chapters of this book for instruction on searching these resources. Cite the U.S. Constitution in this format: U.S. Const. art. IV, § 5(b).

II. Federal Statutes

The United States Code (USC) codifies federal statutes under fifty-four titles. Within each title, individual statutes are assigned section numbers. To cite a federal statute, include both the title and the section number, and insert periods in the code abbreviation. The federal statute granting appellate jurisdiction to federal appellate courts is 28 U.S.C. § 1291 (2018); title 28 is devoted to courts and judicial matters, and 1291 is the section number assigned to this statute. The year 2018 denotes the edition of the code, which contains laws passed through that year, though publication actually occurred in 2019 or later.

The USC is the official codified version of the federal code and is issued in print every six years. Cumulative annual supplements contain laws passed between the six-year editions. An authenticated version is available online from the Government Publishing Office (GPO) at govinfo.gov, a GPO website.

The more commonly used sources for researching federal statutes are commercially produced and extensively annotated: United States Code Service (USCS) on Lexis and United States Code Annotated (USCA) on Westlaw. Both are also available in print in some libraries. Even if you use a commercial source to research a federal statute, try to confirm the text in the official USC (in print or on GPO's website) and cite it.

Both USCA and USCS contain the text of federal statutes, federal court rules, and the U.S. Constitution. They also provide references to related research sources:

- Cases interpreting or applying each federal statute, rule, or the Constitution;
- Secondary sources on related topics;
- Federal regulations and executive orders; and
- Tables listing statutes by popular names.

Traditionally, some researchers felt that USCA provided more case annotations than USCS, while USCS provided better information on court rules and administrative regulations. Often the two are of equal value, so use whichever one is available. When working with these online sources, check the date through which the statute is current; often this information is given at the top of the screen.

III. Federal Legislative Research

The legislative process in Congress is similar to the Oregon legislative process described in Chapter 6. The Library of Congress website at Congress.gov includes a section on "The Legislative Process," with links to detailed videos (and transcripts) explaining each step of the process. Table B.2. shows this process.

Table B.2. Federal Legislative Process

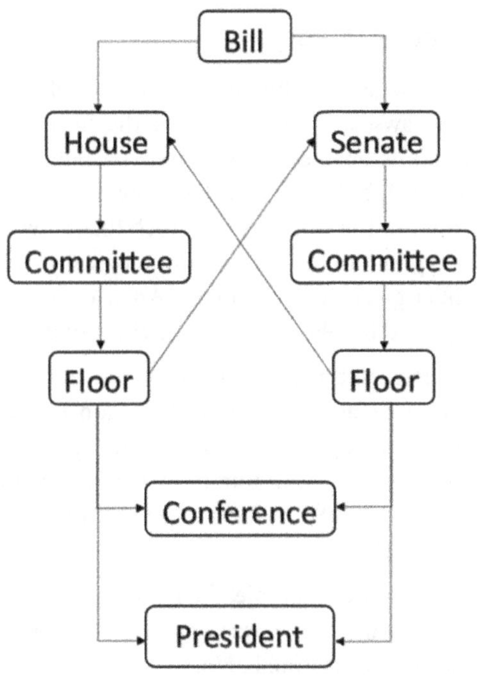

Each Congress meets for two years, in two, year-long sessions that match the calendar year. For example, the 118th Congress held its first session in 2023 and its second session in 2024. Federal bills are numbered sequentially in each chamber of Congress. Generally, Senate bill numbers are preceded by an "S." and House of Representatives bill numbers are preceded by "H.R." A bill that is not enacted in a particular two-year cycle dies and must be re-introduced in the following Congress.

A. Federal Bill Tracking

Much congressional material is available from government websites. The website Congress.gov provides bill summaries and status, committee reports, and the Congressional Record (which records debate in the House and Senate). The website is free and updated daily. It contains material back to 1995. Lexis and Westlaw provide federal bill tracking through databases named "Bill Tracking Report—Current Congress" and "Federal Bill Tracking," respectively. Each has historical bill tracking material available, with varying dates of coverage.

B. Federal Legislative History

Researching federal legislative history involves roughly the same steps as researching Oregon's laws, although some of the terminology is different. When a federal statute is enacted, it is assigned a public law number. This number is in the form Pub. L. No. 101-336, where the numerals before the hyphen are the number of the Congress in which the law was enacted and the numerals after the hyphen are assigned chronologically as bills are enacted. The public law number given above is for the Americans with Disabilities Act (ADA), which was passed in 1990 during the 101st Congress.

The new statute is later published as a session law in United States Statutes at Large, which is the federal counterpart of Oregon Laws. Session laws are designated by volume and page in Statutes at Large, e.g., 104 Stat. 328. Finally, the new statute is assigned a section number when it is codified with statutes on similar topics in the United States Code. The citation for the first section of the ADA is 42 U.S.C. § 12101.

To summarize with another example, the Patient Protection and Affordable Care Act (known as "Obamacare") was enacted in 2010. The bill was H.R. 3590. The public law number is Pub. L. No. 111-148, showing it was the 148th statute enacted in the 111th Congress. Its session law citation is 124 Stat. 119. It is codified at 42 U.S.C. § 18001 et seq.

As with Oregon legislative history, federal legislative history research typically begins with a statute number. If you do not know the statute number, use an annotated code or online service to find it (as described in Chapter 6). With a statute number, you can find the session law citation and public law number, which will lead to the legislative history of the bill as it worked its way through Congress. Table B.3 compares sources for Oregon and federal legislative history.

Table B.3. Sources for Oregon and Federal Legislative History

Action	Oregon Sources	Federal Sources
Committee work	Minutes and audio logs; audio recordings; exhibits of hearings	Committee reports; transcripts, video or livestream of hearings; committee prints
Floor debate and votes	*Journal of the Senate* *Journal of the House*	*Congressional Record*
Session law	*Oregon Laws*	*Statutes at Large*
Codified version	*Oregon Revised Statutes* (official in print, unofficial online) *West's Oregon Revised Statues Annotated* (unofficial in print and online through Westlaw products) Lexis (online only)	United States Code (official) *United States Code Annotated* (West in print and online) *United States Code Service* (Lexis in print and online)

1. Sources of Federal Legislative History

The goal of federal legislative history research is to find committee reports, materials from committee hearings, and transcripts of floor debates. Committee reports are considered the most persuasive authority. Unlike Oregon's committee reports, which are short forms, Congressional committee reports are often lengthy documents. These reports contain the committee's analysis of the bill, the reasons for enacting it, and the views of any committee members who disagree with those reasons. Congressional hearing materials include transcripts from the proceedings and documents such as prepared testimony and exhibits. A committee print may publish the staff's research and supporting documents.

Floor debates are published in the Congressional Record. Be wary in relying on these statements as they represent the views of just one person. Further, the remarks might not have actually been delivered in the House or Senate; members of Congress can amend their remarks and even submit written statements that are published in transcript form as if they were spoken.

2. Compiled Legislative History

Similar to the Oregon archivist staff compiling tracings of certain Oregon statutes, researchers have compiled legislative history for certain federal statutes. A widely known reference book that compiles legislative histories of major federal statutes is Sources of Compiled Legislative Histories, which is available on HeinOnline through the U.S. Federal Legislative History library. It is worthwhile to see whether a compiled legislative history exists before identifying all the documents yourself.

3. Resources for Federal Legislative History

The sites noted earlier in this appendix for tracking federal legislation also provide useful information for legislative history research. The website Congress.gov provides bill summaries, text, amendments, and status; cosponsors and related bills; committee reports; and the Congressional Record. Much federal legislative history is available on Lexis and Westlaw, both in general databases devoted to legislation and in topical databases. In addition, ProQuest Congressional and ProQuest Legislative Insight are two of the most comprehensive sites, with the latter focusing on activity that led to enacted law.

IV. Federal Court Rules

Federal courts have court rules, similar to the rules for Oregon courts. The Federal Rules of Civil Procedure, the Federal Rules of Evidence, and other rules apply to all federal courts, including federal courts in Oregon; they are widely available online as well as in USC, USCS, and USCA. To locate the rules for individual federal courts in Oregon, you may need to consult either comprehensive databases, such as Lexis or Westlaw, or the jurisdiction-specific deskbook *Oregon Rules of Court: Federal*. Additionally, courts frequently post their rules on their websites. For example, rules for the United States District Court for the District of Oregon are on its website, linked from the US Courts website. A well-known treatise on federal rules is *Federal Practice and Procedure*, though many excellent treatises exist.

V. Federal Administrative Law

The federal government's administrative agencies function much like Oregon's. Agencies such as the Civil Rights Division of the Department of Justice, the Internal Revenue Service, and the U.S. Fish and Wildlife Service are invaluable parts of the executive branch. The federal Administrative Procedure Act (APA) is codified at 5 U.S.C. § 551 et seq. Like Oregon's APA, its goals are to promote uniformity, public participation, and public confidence in the fairness of the procedures used by agencies of the federal government.

A. Code of Federal Regulations

Federal administrative rules are called regulations. Federal regulations are published by the Government Publishing Office (GPO) in the Code of Federal Regulations (CFR). Additionally, you can access the CFR at www.ecfr.gov, an unofficial compilation of federal regulations that is kept current daily. The CFR is also available on Lexis and Westlaw, which keep their databases fairly current.

Similar to rules in the OAR in Oregon, regulations in the CFR are organized by agency and subject. The titles of the CFR do not necessarily correspond to the titles of the United States Code (USC), although some subjects do fall under the same title number. For instance, title 7 in both CFR and USC pertain to agriculture, but title 11 of USC addresses bankruptcy, while the same title in the CFR deals with federal elections.

B. Federal Register

New regulations and proposed changes to existing regulations are published in the Federal Register, the federal equivalent of the Oregon Bulletin. The Federal Register is the first source to publish regulations in their final form when they are adopted (i.e., before they are codified in the CFR). In addition to providing the text of regulations, the Federal Register contains notices of hearings, responses to public comments on proposed regulations, executive orders, and helpful tables and indexes. It is published almost every weekday, with continuous pagination throughout the year. This means that citation to page numbers in the thousands is common. The Federal Register is available online through the government sites and on Lexis and Westlaw.

C. Decisions of Federal Agencies

Like Oregon agencies, federal agencies hold quasi-judicial hearings to decide cases that arise under the agencies' regulations. Increasingly, agency decisions are available on agency websites and on Lexis and Westlaw.

VI. Federal Courts and Cases

Table B.4. Federal Court System and Reporters

Court	Reporter Name	Abbreviation
U.S. Supreme Court	*United States Reports* (official), *Supreme Court Reporter*, *United States Supreme Court Reports, Lawyers' Edition*	U.S. S. Ct. L. Ed. or L. Ed. 2d
U.S. Court of Appeals	*Federal Reporter*	F. or F.2d or F.3d or F.4th
U.S. District Court (trial court)	*Federal Supplement*	F. Supp. or F. Supp. 2d or F. Supp. 3d

A. Federal Trial Courts

The trial courts in the federal system are called United States District Courts. There are ninety-four district courts in the federal system, with each district drawn from a particular state. A state with a relatively small population might not be subdivided into smaller geographic regions. The entire state of Oregon, for example, makes up the federal District of Oregon. Even so, district courts are located in three cities: Portland, Eugene, and Medford.

States with larger populations and higher caseloads are subdivided into more districts. For example, California has four federal districts: northern, central, southern, and eastern. Washington has two federal districts: eastern and western.

Selected cases from the United States District Courts, the federal trial courts, are reported in Federal Supplement (abbreviated F. Supp.), published by West and now in its third series. Some opinions from the Federal Supplement series are available on the U.S. Courts website, as well as Google Scholar and other online providers. Lexis and Westlaw tend to make available more U.S. District Court cases, but "unpublished" decisions carry less authoritative weight than those published in Federal Supplement.

B. Federal Circuit Courts of Appeals

Intermediate appellate courts in the federal system are called United States Courts of Appeals. There are courts of appeals for each of the thirteen federal circuits. Twelve of these circuits are based on geographic jurisdiction. Eleven numbered circuits cover groups of states; the twelfth is the District of Columbia Circuit. The thirteenth federal circuit, called the Federal Circuit, hears appeals from district courts in all other circuits on issues related to patent law and from certain specialized courts and agencies.

Oregon is in the Ninth Circuit, so cases from the United States District Court for the District of Oregon are appealed to the United States Court of Appeals for the Ninth Circuit. This circuit encompasses Alaska, Arizona, California, Hawaii, Idaho, Montana, Nevada, Oregon, and Washington, as well as Guam and the Northern Mariana Islands.

Cases decided by the intermediate appellate courts in the federal system are published in West's Federal Reporter, now in its fourth series (F.4th is the reporter abbreviation). Federal appeals courts maintain their own websites that provide access to recent cases for free. The U.S. Courts website provides a gateway to each federal court. Both Lexis and Westlaw include cases from federal courts of appeals in several databases. Other online providers typically provide access to federal appellate cases, too. Some appellate cases that were not selected for publication in Federal Reporter were published by West in Federal Appendix. Additional cases may be available on Lexis and Westlaw. Be careful, however. If a case does not have a citation to Federal Reporter, the case may be of limited authority in some jurisdictions.

C. Supreme Court of the United States

The highest court in the federal system is the United States Supreme Court. It decides cases concerning the United States Constitution and federal statutes. This court does not have the final say on matters of purely state law, unless the state law conflicts with federal law. Parties who wish to have the U.S. Supreme Court hear their cases must file a petition for certiorari, as the court almost always has discretion over which cases it hears.

Decisions of the United States Supreme Court are reported in United States Reports (U.S.), the official reporter; Supreme Court Reporter (S. Ct.), a West publication; and United States Supreme Court Reports, Lawyers' Edition, now in its second series (L. Ed. 2d), published by LexisNexis. Although United States Reports is the official reporter, meaning that you should cite it, if possible, that series frequently publishes cases several years after they are decided. Thus, for recent cases, lawyers often cite the Supreme Court Reporter. You can access a PDF version of United States Reports for many cases on HeinOnline.

There are several free online sources for Supreme Court opinions, including the Court's website, the Cornell Law School's Legal Information Institute, and Google Scholar. Both Lexis and Westlaw provide quick access to Supreme Court opinions, as well as to briefs filed by the parties. The U.S. Courts website contains a map showing the federal circuits and districts, court addresses, explanations of jurisdiction, and other helpful information. The address is www.uscourts.gov. Reporters for cases decided by federal courts are listed above in section VI, along with their national citation abbreviations. Citation to these cases is introduced in Appendix A of this book. Table B.4 lists the reporters for federal cases.

D. Topical Reporters

Some reporters publish cases on a particular topic, rather than cases from a specific court or region. For example, Federal Rules Decisions includes federal trial court cases that analyze federal rules of civil and criminal procedure that do not appear in Federal Supplement. Similarly, West's Bankruptcy Reporter includes cases from United States Bankruptcy Courts, including those in Oregon. West publishes both reporters, so they contain West's editorial enhancements. Other publishers also provide reporters in topical areas. An example is Bloomberg BNA's Media Law Reporter, which publishes all relevant opinions of the United States Supreme Court as well as significant opinions of federal and state courts on the topic of media law.

About the Authors

Megan Austin is the Law Instruction Librarian at the University of Oregon Law Library. She teaches legal research to law students and undergraduates. She received her J.D. and M.L.I.S. from the University of Arizona.

Kelly Reynolds is a Law Reference Librarian at the University of Oregon Law Library. She teaches legal research and provides consultations for student and faculty research. She received her J.D. from Brigham Young University and her M.L.I.S. from the University of North Texas.

Index

See "Terms of art" for pages where legal words or phrases are defined or are introduced for the first time. Often, they will be italicized, in bold, or in quotation marks to make finding them easy.

Most index entries dealing solely with federal research sources and processes appear under the heading "Federal research."